DEMYSTIFYING

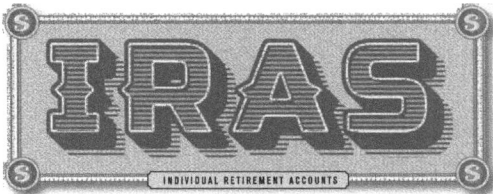

IRAS

INDIVIDUAL RETIREMENT ACCOUNTS

DEMYSTIFYING

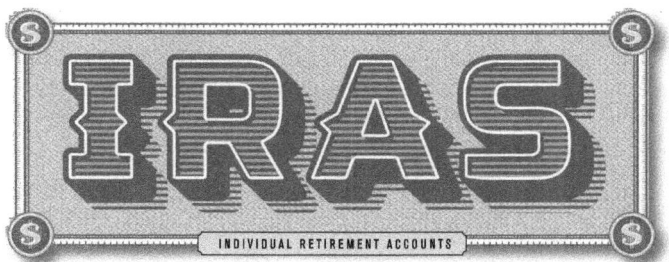

IRAS

INDIVIDUAL RETIREMENT ACCOUNTS

A User's Guide to
Tax-qualified Money

MICHAEL TOVE

FUTURE
PUBLISHING

SOUTHFIELD, MI

■FUTURE
■PUBLISHING

Published by Future Publishing
Southfield, MI

Publisher's Cataloging-in-Publication Data
Tove, Michael.

Demystifying IRAS : a user's guide to tax-qualified money / Michael Tove. –
Southfield, MI : Future Pub., 2020.

p. ; cm.

ISBN13: 978-1-970114-09-6

1. Individual retirement accounts--United States. 2. Individual retirement
accounts--Taxation--United States. 3. Individual retirement accounts--Law and
legislation--United States. 4. Retirement income--United States. I. Title.

HG1660.U5 T68 2020
332.02401--dc23   2020908283

Project coordination by Jenkins Group, Inc. • www.BookPublishing.com

Printed in the United States of America
24 23 22 21 20 • 5 4 3 2 1

CONTENTS

Chapter 1

HISTORY OF THE IRA

The "Individual Retirement Account" (IRA) was invented as part of ERISA (Employee Retirement Income Security Act) and signed into law by President Gerald Ford on Labor Day 1974. The idea was to encourage workers to accumulate money, tax-deferred, while at high income tax brackets until retirement when they would be at lower tax brackets. The purpose was to relieve the burden on Social Security by creating an individual savings incentive that would supplement Social Security with an additional source of retirement income.

When introduced, the plan was attractive. In 1974, the top marginal tax bracket was 70% (for an individual earning at least $100,000; $200,000 for couples filing jointly). At that time, the average annual income was less than $10,000 and those income-earners faced a top marginal bracket of 25%. However, Social Security was not taxed so retirees enjoyed a substantial drop in taxable income compared with their working years. Therefore, deferring tax on income until retirement provided a significant benefit, especially for the higher wage-earners.

Then times changed. In 1981, President Ronald Reagan pushed through a massive tax reduction act which lowered the top marginal bracket to 50% (individuals earning $41,500; couples earning $85,600). By then, the average annual income had increased by a third and was close to $15,000 with those filers remaining at 25%. In 1984, Social Security benefits started to be taxed. In 1987, another tax reduction act reduced the top marginal bracket to 38.5% ($54,000 for individuals; $90,000 for couples). While the average annual income had increased to about $18,500, those tax filers now faced a top marginal bracket of 15%.

In other words, from 1974 through 1987, the average annual income increased by more than 85% while tax rates fell by 60% and tax on Social Security appeared. Retirees living on a combination of Social Security, pensions plus other income secondary sources, increasingly saw no reduction of taxable income in retirement. Thus, where in 1974, the tax deferral logic of an IRA was strong, just 13 years later, it was not.

However, to this day, tax-deferred IRAs and their "kin" (collectively known as qualified money) have remained popular. In fact, according to a report by the Investment Company Institute (ICI), at the end of the first quarter 2017, there was approximately $26.1 trillion held in various qualified retirement accounts.

In 1974, workers accumulated tax-deferred qualified money as a primary source of future retirement income. Today, retirees commonly do not regard their IRAs as a primary source of retirement income and because of taxes, dread the inevitable liquidation schedule of required minimum distributions (RMDs). Unfortunately, all the IRS sees is $26.1 trillion that's never been taxed and they want "their money." That creates a conflict between the retiree (who does not need the money and does not want to pay taxes) and the IRS (who does).

The purpose of this book is to examine IRA concepts and strategies, and among other things, help individuals to discover strategies that may help them minimize—or even eliminate—tax exposure on income in retirement and beyond (inheritance). One of the fundamental goals of good financial planning is to take advantage of prudent tax avoidance strategies because...

It's not how much you make that counts but how much you get to keep.

Reducing tax exposure increases the total effective income, even if the raw amount doesn't change.

However, it is critical to draw a distinction between tax avoidance which is legal and tax evasion, which is not. These distinctions are firmly rooted in American legal precedent:

"Anyone may so arrange his affairs that his taxes shall be as low as possible; he is not bound to choose that pattern which will best pay the Treasury; there is not even a patriotic duty to increase one's taxes."

– Judge Learned Hand: Helvering v. Gregory, 69 F.2d 809 (2d Cir. 1934).

This seminal quote from Judge Hand is sometimes cited as a cause to avoid paying taxes... by people who never read the actual case. It's a perfect example of relying on assumptions which are untrue, or worse, half-true.

The case for which Judge Hand wrote this opinion revolved around a dispute between the IRS and Mrs. Evelyn Gregory, who privately owned three corporations. The first, United Mortgage Company, was her principal company, of which

Mrs. Gregory owned 100% of the stock. The other two were, in effect, shell corporations, both of which she also was sole owner. In 1928, Mrs. Gregory transferred stock from United Mortgage to Monitor Securities Corporation, then three days later to Averill Corporation. She then sold the stock from Averill and deducted $10,000 ($147,000 in today's dollars) of the gains as tax-free corporate restructuring.

IRS Commissioner Guy Helvering disagreed, arguing that because Mrs. Gregory was sole owner of all three corporations, she was merely moving money from one to the next. Accordingly, there was no actual restructuring and therefore no allowable deduction. Mrs. Gregory sued and the Board of Tax Appeals (today's Tax Court) ruled in her favor. Helvering appealed to the United States Court of Appeals for the Second Circuit (New York), which was presided over by Judge Learned Hand. Judge Hand is often regarded as the finest jurist never to have served on the U.S. Supreme Court.

Judge Hand's quote (above) was from his written opinion that unanimously represented the Court. However, the opinion continued to state that any time a sequence of transactions, even if each separately lawful, is combined to produce an effect that in total is contrary to the law (including intent), the entire transaction is invalid. In other words, Judge Hand and the Court ruled *in favor* of Helvering (and the IRS). Mrs. Gregory appealed to the U.S. Supreme Court which in 1935 unanimously upheld the Second Circuit. To this day, this case stands as a precedent for the doctrine of substance over form.

It is sometimes said that...

> *There are two sets of laws in the United States:*
> *One for the informed and one for everyone else.*

This book will explore a variety of the "informed" set of laws and propose some strategies to take advantage of those.

However, nothing in this book is intended to replace professional tax, legal or financial advice. Anyone seeking specific, personal solutions should contact the appropriately licensed professional. The laws in all these areas can be complex and are continually changing. In addition, many solutions for planning require advanced knowledge and access to resources available only through those licensed professionals. They may also be state-specific. It is for these reasons that it is ill-advised for anyone to attempt to make decisions without professional advice. So yes, this is an informative "how to" book. But that objective is intended more to function in an educational capacity rather than offering finite personal solutions. Accordingly, it is strongly recommended that any solution discussed herein is also discussed with your advisor professional to determine if that strategy is best *for you*.

Before proceeding, one more important distinction must be made: Any discussion herein about taxation refers exclusively to income tax. Other taxes exist, most notably estate or inheritance tax which, in 2020, applies only to individuals who die with a net worth in excess of $11.58 million. Presently, that exemption limit is scheduled to drop in 2026. What future action Congress may take with respect to this tax is highly speculative at best. However, regardless of what transpires in the future, these are separate planning issues and not part of the discussion herein.

Chapter 2

BASIC IRA RULES

With limited exceptions, contributions to IRAs are made with pre-tax dollars. That means, if the contribution comes from your paycheck or directly from your employer, no income tax is withheld and no income tax is due on that money for that tax year. The money then gets to grow deferred from income tax until such time when it is withdrawn. Of course at that time, the money received is reported as ordinary taxable income.

There are also restrictions on withdrawals:

1. Withdrawals from an IRA prior to age 59½ are not permitted. Doing so generates not only a taxable consequence on the money withdrawn but also incurs a 10% tax penalty. There are however, a few transactions for which the 10% penalty is waived:

    a. **First-Time Home Purchase** – IRA owners younger than 59½ may withdraw up to $10,000 per individual ($20,000 per couple) without incurring the 10% tax penalty for the purchase of a home. However, it must be a "FIRST" home, not an "upgrade." Technically you must not have owned a home in the last two years. The money received is still taxable as ordinary income but is forgiven the 10% penalty. In other words, a first-time home buyer who is taxed at 12% and withdraws $10,000 gets to "keep" $8,800 after taxes. However, that's a lot better than the $7,920 which would be "kept" if the 10% tax penalty is also included. If however, the home purchase is cancelled or delayed, the money must be replaced back in the IRA within 120 days to avoid the penalty. Also, withdrawing more than the allowed amount, even if otherwise qualified, will incur a 10% penalty on the excess.

b. **Disability** – By definition, a person is disabled if he or she is "*unable to engage in any substantial gainful activity by reason of any medically determinable physical or mental impairment which can be expected to result in death or to be of long-continued and indefinite duration.*" A person who becomes disabled younger than 59½ may withdraw from any tax-qualified account without paying the 10% tax penalty. However, the IRS will require proof from a licensed physician or medical practitioner.

c. **Medical Expenses** – Distributions from tax qualified plans avoid the 10% penalty if they are used to pay for medical expenses not reimbursed by insurance, provided those expenses exceed 10% of person's Adjusted Gross Income (AGI). For example, a person with $50,000 total income and more than $5000 in uninsured medical expenses may use the IRA without paying the penalty. However, the money withdrawn is still subject to ordinary income tax.

d. **Health Insurance Premiums** (from IRA only) – Withdrawals to pay health insurance premiums avoid the tax penalty if a person is unemployed and certain additional conditions are met:

- Unemployment compensation is received for at least 12 consecutive weeks.
- The withdrawal is made the year unemployment compensation is received or the subsequent year.
- The withdrawal was made at least 60 days before employment at a new job.

e. **Higher Education Expenses** (IRA only) – Withdrawals to DIRECTLY PAY a higher education facility for yourself, your spouse, your child or your grandchild avoid the 10% penalty. Qualified higher education expenses may include tuition at a postsecondary school (e.g., college, university, trade school), room and board (if enrolled at least half-time), books, fees, supplies and equipment that may be required by the institution for enrollment or attendance.

f. **Military Service** – Members of the armed forces, if active duty for at least 179 days, may withdraw from an IRA without paying the 10% penalty.

g. **72(t) Distributions** – IRS Code 72(t) permits penalty-free distributions of an IRA prior to age 59½ IF those payments occur as at least five years of "Substantially Equal, Periodic Distributions." Essentially, 72(t) distributions must occur from an annuity as nothing else qualifies. More on annuities later, but simply put, an annuity is an account with an insurance company. Specific to Rule 72(t), those distributions must be scheduled through the annuity contract and not occur as discretionary cash withdrawals.

h. **Qualified Adoptions** – Effective January 1, 2020, new law permits penalty-free withdrawals from retirement plans by the plan owner for the birth or adoption of a child.

i. **Inherited IRA** – If you inherit an IRA from someone other than your spouse, you are required to start withdrawals no later than the year after the year of death. Your age has nothing to do with it so there is no 10% withdrawal penalty. You may not combine an inherited IRA with your own. (See also Chapter 10. Inherited IRAs). If you inherit an IRA from a spouse, you may combine that IRA with your own. If you elect to do that, then the rules of withdrawal are the same as they are for your own IRA, including the 10% penalty if you withdraw funds prior to 59½.

There is an additional group of manipulations for which not only is the 10% penalty waived but also can occur without generating a taxable consequence.

"**Rollover**" – This is a transfer from one IRA to another. This term is frequently used to describe two different transaction strategies for that purpose.

- **(True) Rollover** – A rollover occurs when the IRA is liquidated to the IRA owner, thereby triggering a potential tax event unless the transfer meets two specific conditions:
  a. The rollover must be completed meaning the money is returned to another IRA in not more than 60 days from the date the liquidation check was cut.
  b. No other rollover has occurred in the preceding 12 months.

- **Direct Transfer** – This is the transfer of an IRA directly from institution to institution, without the money ever being liquidated directly to the IRA owner. Direct transfer rollovers can also be used to convert an account from one type of qualified plan (e.g., 401(k) plan) to another (e.g., traditional IRA).

If the transfer is completed under these provisions, then no income tax on the transferred amount is due and no 10% penalty is imposed. However, a Direct Transfer is a safer method because it has none of the time or frequency limitations of a Rollover.

Roth Conversion – Anyone with a traditional IRA or other qualified plan may convert that plan to a Roth IRA. Regardless of age, the 10% Penalty is waived but the transaction is a taxable event at ordinary income tax rates. As will be discussed later, there are times when this manipulation may be advantageous and times when it is not.

Specialty Plans – There are a few tax qualified plans that permit money to grow and be received tax-free. These plans are funded with after-tax dollars but the growth is tax-exempt upon receipt provided the money is used for its intended purpose. Failure to withdraw the money properly can result in both a tax load plus the 10% penalty. The two most common are 529 and HSA plans.

529 Plan – This is a college savings plan. Contributions are invested and grow tax-free provided the funds are used to pay for higher education. However, anyone may have a 529 plan and anyone may contribute to someone else's 529 plan. Access is easy and flexible. Withdrawals are permitted for any reasonable expense associated with higher education (after high school), whether college, university, trade school, or even for qualified apprentice-ships, some primary school and even home schooling and up to $10,000 of qualified student loan repayments including for siblings. Allowed withdrawals also include tuition, room and board, books and lab fees and any required equipment (e.g., computers, calculators, etc.) necessary for that education. 529 plans are designated state-by-state and using the in-state 529 plan can qualify for not only elimination of federal income tax exposure, but also state income tax exposure (where levied). Some states offer reciprocal agreements meaning they extend state income tax exemption for 529 plans from any state.

HSA Plan – HSA stands for health savings account. These accounts are paired with high deductible medical insurance plans. The funds are invested, grow tax-exempt and are received tax-free if used for major medical expense (hence the high deductible pairing). The idea is to net reduce the cost of medical insurance to the individual. HSA funds withdrawn for other than medical expense are taxable and potentially subject to the 10% tax penalty.

Required Minimum Distributions

When an IRA owner reaches the required beginning age (RBA), a mandatory liquidation schedule is imposed. Prior to January 1, 2020, the required beginning age was 70½. However, in December 2019, the SECURE Act (**S**etting **E**very **C**ommunity **U**p for **RE**tirement) was signed into law. Anyone who turned 70½ by or before December 31, 2019, will remain on the old distribution schedule. Anyone who turns 70½ after that date will have their required beginning age deferred until age 72.

a. **Standard RMD Table (Table III)** – Most retirees have their RMDs calculated from this method. Essentially, it is a table of divisors each corresponding to a person's age as of December 31 of the current tax year. Presently (2020) the former RMD table applies to all RMDs regardless of starting age.

Age	Divisor	Age	Divisor	Age	Divisor	Age	Divisor
70	27.4	82	17.1	94	9.1	106	4.2
71	26.5	83	16.3	95	8.6	107	3.9
72	25.6	84	15.5	96	8.1	108	3.7
73	24.7	85	14.8	97	7.6	109	3.4
74	23.8	86	14.1	98	7.1	110	3.1
75	22.9	87	13.4	99	6.7	111	2.9
76	22.0	88	12.7	100	6.3	112	2.6
77	21.2	89	12.0	101	5.9	113	2.4
78	20.3	90	11.4	102	5.5	114	2.1
79	19.5	91	10.8	103	5.2	115+	1.9
80	18.7	92	10.2	104	4.9		
81	17.9	93	9.6	105	4.5		

However, in the fall of 2019, the IRS published a new table. It has not (as of the date of writing) taken effect but seems likely to do so in the future, probably by or before 2022 when persons turning 70 in 2020 will start their RMDs at age 72.

Age	Divisor	Age	Divisor	Age	Divisor	Age	Divisor
70	29.1	83	17.6	96	8.3	109	3.7
71	28.2	84	16.8	97	7.8	110	3.5
72	27.3	85	16.0	98	7.3	111	3.4
73	26.4	86	15.2	99	6.8	112	3.2
74	25.5	87	14.4	100	6.4	113	3.1
75	24.6	88	13.6	101	5.9	114	3.0
76	23.7	89	12.9	102	5.6	115	2.9
77	22.8	90	12.1	103	5.2	116	2.8
78	21.9	91	11.4	104	4.9	117	2.7
79	21.0	92	10.8	105	4.6	118	2.5
80	20.2	93	10.1	106	4.3	119	2.3
81	19.3	94	9.5	107	4.1	120+	2.0
82	18.4	95	8.9	108	3.9		

The applicable RMD is calculated by dividing the IRA account value as of December 31 of the previous year, by the applicable factor (called the "distribution period") at the IRA owner's actual age on December 31 of the current year. This is the amount of money which must be liquidated. It is reported as taxable income at ordinary income tax rates. Failure to take a RMD incurs a 50% tax penalty, plus interest. Even if under appeal, the IRS waives the 50% penalty, they cannot waive any interest accrued.

Except for the first year, RMDs must be taken by December 31 of the tax year for which that distribution will be reported. That continues every year until the IRA is completely liquidated. First year RMDs may be delayed until April 1 of the following year but doing so invites two "tax traps."

First, waiting past December 31 means that in the second year, two RMDs will be taken in a single year. Not only does this increase the taxable income by two RMDs, potentially incurring a higher marginal tax bracket for some of that distribution, it may result in an increase of how much Social Security income is taxed.

Second, it results in a form of double taxation on a portion of the IRA. The reason is that by waiting past December 31 to take the first RMD, that first RMD is now also included in the second RMD. In other words, you must take an RMD on some of the same money twice. For example: Assume you have an IRA worth $100,000. At age 72 (new table) your RMD is $3,663. If you take that RMD on or before December 31, then your age 72 RMD is reduced by that amount and your 2nd RMD (for age 73) is calculated on $96,337 or $3,649. But waiting until after December 31 to take your first RMD now, means your age 73 RMD is calculated on $100,000 or $3,788. In other words, delaying past December 31 to take the first RMD *increased* the second RMD by $139 for no reason other than you delayed. You may argue that the added tax on $139 isn't all that much ($30.58 if at the 22% marginal bracket), but who out there would voluntarily make a $30.58 charitable donation to the IRS? Money is money. By the way, do you still pick up loose change when you find it?

   b. **Table II.** When the ages of an IRA owner and spouse differ by more than ten years, there is a different table which discounts the size of the RMDs to the older spouse. These discounts do not apply to the younger spouse because the standard RMD table is more favorable for the younger spouse.

   c. **Rule 72(t) Distributions**. When an IRA is liquidated according to Rule 72(t), that payment schedule substitutes for the standard RMD table. An IRA owner does not have to take both.

   d. **Table I** is a life expectancy table. When an IRA owner dies, and the IRA's beneficiary is not the IRA owner's spouse, it must be liquidated as an inherited IRA. If certain specific conditions are met, an inherited IRA may be liquidated according to this life expectancy table. This table of inherited IRA distributions is much more favorable than any of the others, especially when IRA beneficiaries are young. However, there are a number of potential obstacles to being able to take advantage of this schedule. For more details, see Chapter 10: Inheriting IRAs.

Knowing how RMDs work and the tax implications are important tools for planning. Knowledge is power and being able to take advantage of tax reduction strategies can lead to smart planning. However, guard against becoming overly obsessed with tax avoidance and...

Don't let the tax tail wag the dog.

Sometimes, there's advantage in accepting a bit of tax exposure. It's not about what to avoid as much as what the benefit in exchange for the trade-off really is.

The Power of Tax-deferred Growth

One of the biggest advantages of an IRA is tax-deferred growth, the value of which is not to be underestimated. Albert Einstein is quoted as having said "*The greatest force in the universe is compound interest.*" This is correct. But what do people do in "real life"? Far too often, they watch their accounts day-by-day and judge success after a few weeks or a couple of months, never seeing the value of the LONG-TERM.

To illustrate this point, let's play a little game. For our purposes here, just respond as though the game were real and don't try to second guess the "motives."

Suppose you're offered a temporary job; eight hours per day for 30 consecutive days with no days off. Your salary is two cents per day. Would you even consider the job? Probably not but let's assume you do. If you agree to work and not quit, after two days, you'll get a raise equal to what you've earned so far. Would you now accept the job?

Assume you do accept:

On Day 1, you earn (as promised), two cents ($0.02)

On Day 2, you earn another two cents for a grand total of four cents ($0.04).

On Day 3, you get a raise to $0.04 per day so at the end of Day 3, you have earned a grand total of $0.08.

By Day 10, you have earned a grand total of $10.24 which translates to 12.8 cents per hour. What do you think about the job now? Are you toying with the idea of just quitting?

At this point, you are offered a $10,000 buy-out. In other words, you could quit and get paid $10,000 for ten days work. You just got paid $1,000 per day. That's not so bad is it? What would you do? What would your friends tell you to do? Would you make this decision alone or would you ask them for advice?

Let's assume you decide to continue the original job. By Day 15 (half way through), you have earned a "whopping" $327.68. That's just $2.73 per hour! Of course, you could still take the $10,000 buy-out although now you just worked for five days for nothing. Suppose at this moment, you're offered another job. It's identical work for the next 15 days but pays $1,000 per day. Suddenly, your world is rosy. You could take the $10,000 buy-out, switch and pick up another $15,000. You're $25,000 richer in just one month! Do you earn anything close to that in your "regular" job? Would you switch to get the $25,000 or would you stick to the first job even though your total actual earning so far is just $327.68. What would you do?

Regardless of your responses to the game, this scenario of second-guessing in light of distractions is not unlike what investors commonly face every day. People have a tendency to be impatient for results, not trusting the long-term strategy and not fully accepting that a plan designed to span years cannot be judged on the basis of days, weeks or even months. The more people watch their long-term retirement accounts like a hawk, trying to second guess what tomorrow's markets will do, the more susceptible they become to short-term distractions. Research (and there's plenty of it) consistently shows that active traders who try to beat the markets usually do far worse than less aggressive investors who set and stick to a long-term plan.

Markets fluctuate up and down. That's what they do but the value of a long-term plan is that those short-term oscillations average out and ultimately don't really matter as much as people fear. And unfortunately, succumbing to short-term distractions is far more costly than what most people realize.

Back to the game: Did you succumb to the distractions? Did you not play because two cents per day is stupid? Did you take the buyout on day 10 and quit? Did you delay to day 15, take the buyout and switch? Did you "stick it out" for the full 30 days? If you did stick it out, why? Was it because you *knew* where this was going or did you suspect there was a "trick" that was going to produce an unexpected result – even if you didn't fully know why? Honestly answer these questions. Think about your reasoning before reading on to learn the answer.

Take one more minute to think about
why you made the choices you did.

If you had stuck to the original job and worked the full 30 days, your total earnings after one month (30 days) would be $10,737,418.24! That's more than 10.7 million dollars! Surprised? That's the power of time and compounding. It took time for the compounding (daily doubling in this case) to "pick up speed" but toward the end of the 30 days, it got very big very fast. If you're skeptical, simply get a calculator and see for yourself: 1 cent doubled, then doubled, then doubled, etc. for a total 30 times is $10,737,418.24 (I "gave" you the first doubling without exactly saying so).

Okay, so you're probably thinking "*Nobody's going to double money every day.*" I agree. But conceptually, in the "real world," the MATH is the same and many people never fully appreciate how significant it is.

So here's a "real world" example. In 1626, Dutch Colonist Pieter Minuit purchased Manhattan Island (New York City) from the Lenape Indians for trade goods valued then at 60 Guilders. That was the dollar equivalent of about $24 or a little more than $1,300 at modern rates. If the Indians had invested the money and earned just 6% per year, today that investment would be worth about $11.5 trillion; more than enough to buy New York City back!

So what impact does taxation have on this process? The answer is shockingly far greater than you might imagine. From our game above, let's assume the earnings are taxed daily at 20% and only the after-tax amount is allowed to double. By the end of the 30 days, your total after-tax earnings would be only $13,292.28. That's 13 thousand dollars; not 10.7 million! So what happened to the "missing" $10,724,125.96? It never existed. The constant erosion of taxation prevented it from ever getting large. *That's* the power of tax-deferred growth.

Chapter 3

TYPES OF IRAS

There are many different versions of the "IRA" including some that significantly predate the 1974 creation of the "Individual Retirement Account." As previously noted, the more appropriate (and technically correct) name for these programs are "tax qualified plans" or simply "qualified plans." Except for Roth IRA, qualified plans are funded with pre-tax dollars and must be liquidated in most cases, starting at a required beginning age (whether 70½ or 72). In order to better understand these plans, it is first necessary to understand a bit about the various versions of qualified plans and how they differ. What is left becomes a common basis for understanding them all.

Tax qualified plans can be broadly categorized as either:

- Employer-sponsored
- Self-directed (set up and funded independently of an employer)

Most people are familiar with employer-sponsored plans, particularly the 401(k). But, before delving into what exactly a 401(k) plan really is, let's consider the broader scope. There are two basic types of employer-sponsored retirement plans:

- **Defined Benefit Plans**
- **Defined Contribution Plans**

A **Defined Benefit Plan** is one where the employer establishes a retirement plan that guarantees a lifetime of income for the employee after he or she retires. These plans are called **pensions**.

A pension is the nation's oldest employer-based retirement plan. First introduced in 1875 by the American Express Company, pension plans remained relatively uncommon through the start of the Great Depression. Where, prior to 1930, just 397 private pension plans existed in the United States and Canada, one decade later, 15% of all private-sector workers were covered by a pension. Over the next half century, a score and a half changes to tax code modified them significantly.

The value of a defined benefit plan is that it establishes, with certainty, how much *income* an employee will receive in retirement for life. The greatest benefit of a pension is that it eliminates any risk that person could ever outlive his or her retirement income. Unfortunately, starting in the 1990's and especially after the Dot-Com market crash in 2000, the cost of maintaining these future lifetime guarantees became increasingly burdensome for employers. As a result, there was a major corporate shift away from defined benefit plans to defined contribution plans.

A **Defined Contribution Plan** is one where the employer only promises how much money they (the employer) will contribute (typically a percentage of an employee's salary), often *after* the employee has contributed to the plan. Worse is that the employer often reserves the right to change that promise or even eliminate it. Essentially, the goal of a defined contribution plan is to encourage an employee to grow a bag of money on his or her own. It is intended to relieve the employer from a lifetime income promise that can no longer be made. It's then up to the retiree to (hopefully) convert that plan into retirement income. Unfortunately, 401(k) plans make no promise or guarantee of how big that bag of money might be, or even that there will be any money at all, and employers generally offer no guidance on how to convert that bag of money into a lifetime pension after the employee retires.

In 2014, Nobel Prize-winning Economist Robert Merton published a scathing rebuke of the shift from defined benefit to defined contribution plans. (*"The Crisis in Retirement Planning,"* Harvard Business Review, July-August 2014). To paraphrase Merton, corporate America shifted its message from *"We'll take care of you for the rest of your life, guaranteed,"* to *"Good luck with that and don't let the door hit you on the way out."*

According to a February 26, 2018 report by Brendon McFarland, (www.towerswatson.com/en/Insights/Newsletters/Americas/Insider/2018/02/evolution-of-retirement-plans-in-fortune-500-companies) only 16% of Fortune 500 companies that offered pensions in 1998, still offered them in 2017.

To be fair, the primary reason for this shift was that the expense and risk of maintaining the defined benefit promise simply became too great for most employers to sustain. It forced their hand but that doesn't help the retiree who is struggling to make ends meet and has no reliable advice on how to do it.

Most defined benefit plans were (are) offered by large corporate employers. If you're fortunate enough to be employed by a company that still offers one, you are likely in a better place than if employed by someone who doesn't. However, check with your human resources representative to make sure you're doing what you can to take full advantage of the offering. From the company's perspective, it is part of your total compensation package and not taking full advantage is as though you asked for a reduced salary.

412(i) Plan – This is a defined-benefit pension plan specifically designed for small business owners. Contributions are tax-deductible to the employer and tax-deferred to the employee. These plans must include a combination of annuities and/or whole life insurance that will administer the pension payments after the employee retires. Developed for small business owners commonly with 10 or fewer employees, the premium requirements are larger than other plans and may be unaffordable, especially those that are not well established. In addition, over the years, there have been multiple cases of abuse in regard to these plans and they remain relatively rare as a component in the overall defined benefit plan space.

See also **Defined Benefit KEOGH Plans** (below)

Employer-Sponsored Defined Contribution Plans

Anytime an employee is offered a defined contribution plan, especially if the employer offers matching money, the employee should participate in the plan. In addition, the employee would be well served to contribute enough of his or her salary to receive the maximum offered match. However, unless there are extenuating circumstances such as you plan to work *for that employer* past age 72 or in your state that plan includes special tax advantages, contributing excess to your plan may not be in your best interest. The reason is that these plans can carry severe restrictions on investment choice and access to the funds. If you have sufficient income to afford more than the minimum contributions you may be better served by investing in a plan under your control. It could be an individual IRA, a Roth IRA or simply a non-qualified investment. In other words...

> *Contribute only the minimum amount necessary*
> *to get the maximum employer match.*

Types of Defined Contribution Plans

401(k) Plan – This is the most popular and wide-spread employer-sponsored retirement plan in existence today.

Invented by Congress under the Revenue Act of 1978, this plan came about almost by accident. The Act introduced a simple provision that allowed employer contributions to be untaxed in the year of contribution, making them very attractive to employers seeking to maximize benefits to employees at minimal cost to themselves. The new provision amended Section 401(k) of the Internal Revenue Code, thereby creating the popular name 401(k) plan.

Typical 401(k) plans permit an employee to divert a portion of his or her salary into the plan and not be taxed on those funds until years later when the plan is liquidated. Similarly, the employer may make a contribution which to them is also tax-deferred.

The philosophy of a 401(k) is similar to the traditional IRA in that presumably, the employee retires at a lower income tax bracket than while working. It also offers the benefit of tax-deferred compounding which as has already been demonstrated, can provide a very substantial benefit. However, the investment choices are generally limited to a short menu of choices, usually mutual funds and many employers impose secondary restrictions on access prior to retirement.

In some cases, employer-limitations have resulted in disastrous consequences. Most notably, prior to November 2001, employees of Enron Corporation were pressed to invest their 401(k) contributions in Enron Common Stock. According to eventual plaintiffs, those contributions came at highly inflated prices. As the financial scandal unfolded, the price of Enron stock plunged, eventually wiping out an estimated $850 billion of employee retirement money.

Currently, there are a number of specific variants on the 401(k), each differing with regard to rules about vesting schedules and access, transferability and so forth. In some cases, those variations are derived from provisions in the tax code and in other cases, they are individual decisions made by the employer's plan administrators. The array of differences is beyond the scope of this book but suffice it to say that specific details about any particular 401(k) plan should be obtained directly from the plan administrator.

Any money that is contributed, whether by you (the employee) directly from your paycheck or by your employer (matching), is tax-deferred. This means that neither you nor your employer is taxed on those contributions. This is a good thing for both of you at the time. However, while for your employer, those non-taxable contributions always remain non-taxable, in your case, the tax holiday only continues until your schedule of RMDs begins. In this regard, 401(k) plans are identical to IRAs with one potential big advantage.

If you continue to work *for the employer that offers the 401(k) (or 403(b) plan)* after reaching your required beginning age, you are permitted to defer your RMDs until you retire. With traditional IRAs, including 401(k) plans from previous employers, RMDs must start at your required beginning age regardless of your employment status. Thus, for those employees who continue to work past their RBA, the 401(k) continues to grow tax-deferred until the point of retirement.

403(b) Plan - Also known as a tax-sheltered annuity or TSA, this plan was invented in 1958 as the first defined contribution plan. The original purpose was to offer certain 501(c) (3) organizations a way to contribute to employee retirement plans on a tax-deferred basis. The provisions for this arrangement appeared in Section 403(b) in the U.S. Tax Code, thereby providing the basis for their common name.

403(b) plans differ from 401(k) plans in two significant ways: 1) they are only available to certain non-profit organizations such as most churches, educational entities (public schools, colleges and universities) and to qualified not-for-profit companies, 2) their administrative costs tend to be less than that of a 401(k). However, short of picking who your employer is, you cannot choose whether you get a 403(b) or 401(k).

Occasionally, clients will ask if they should "open" a 401(k) or 403(b) plan. The short answer is "No." Those plans are strictly offered through qualified employers and generally by larger corporations. However, there are a series of 401(k)-like plans that are available to small employers or even self-employed persons.

SEP (Simplified Employee Pension) – This plan is a variant of a traditional IRA that is offered by a small employer including (especially) a self-employed business owner. The employee is immediately 100% vested meaning there is no artificial limitation on when the funds can be accessed (beyond the standard 59½ limitation). Two of the biggest advantages to the SEP include eligibility requirements that are relaxed compared with other defined contribution plans and contribution limits that are higher than traditional IRAs. In addition, self-employed persons (including sole proprietors) can shelter a lot of income from taxes by contributing to a SEP, and deducting those contributions from current income. For example, as of 2020, SEP contributions are limited to the lesser of 25% of an employee's compensation (including the business owner) or $57,000. By comparison, deductible contributions to a traditional IRA (2020) are limited to $6,000 ($7,000 for persons 50 and older). In addition, employers may skip making annual SEP contributions, for example, during years when business is down. SEPs are especially valuable for self-employed persons who earn very large incomes. Making the SEP contribution permits a tax deduction when high income would result in a significant tax load. Since the Tax Reform Act of 2018, this is especially significant because the number of other available deductions has been reduced.

SIMPLE (Savings **I**ncentive **M**atch **PL**an for Employees) **IRAs** are another IRA variant designed to benefit the small business owner. Less costly to administer, SIMPLEs are not subject to ERISA rules. While like other qualified plans in that they can be funded with pretax dollars, those contributions are still subject to Social Security, Medicare and Federal Unemployment taxes. Also, compared with 401(k) Plans, etc., maximum contribution limits are typically lower.

KEOGH Plans (HR10 Plans) - Established in 1962 and

named after the bill's sponsor, Congressman Eugene James Keogh, these are tax-deferred pension plans available to self-employed individuals or unincorporated businesses. They may be established as either defined benefit or defined contribution plans, although usually, it's the latter.

KEOGH as Defined Benefit Plan – The plan determines an annual amount of benefit to be received at retirement, usually based on salary, and contributions are adjusted to meet that goal. Variables that are included in the calculation are employee age (at planned retirement), projected life expectancy and investment performance. One advantage is that contribution limits are very high. For example the maximum annual contribution (2020) is 100% of salary up to $230,000.

KEOGH as Defined Contribution Plan – The plan determines an allowable (to a limit) amount of contribution to one of two variants:

Profit-Sharing Plan allows a business to contribute up to the lesser of 25% of annual compensation or $57,000 (2020).

Money Purchase Plan, less flexible than profit-sharing, requires a business to contribute a fixed percentage of income every year as specified in the plan documents. Maximum contribution limits are the same as the profit-sharing plan.

For an employer, the defined contribution approach is less complex and therefore less expensive. For an employee, the defined benefit approach offers a better benefit and is more attractive.

Traditional IRA - All the preceding types of qualified plans are provided by employers; even those by self-employed persons.

But an individual may also have an IRA that has nothing to do with his or her employer. These traditional IRAs may be established by:

- Contributing to an individual (or self-directed) IRA or
- "Rolling over" an employer-sponsored plan (usually from a former employer) into an individual IRA.

Establishing and Contributing to an Individual (Traditional) IRA

Individuals may create their own personal IRAs by contributing money to them and taking a deduction for that contribution. Where small business owners get to enjoy this benefit from a SEP, those plans are not available to someone who has no income from self-employment. This is where a traditional IRA can be used.

As of 2020, an individual may contribute up to $6,000 per year to a traditional IRA, with a $1,000 "catch-up" (meaning extra money) if 50 or older. However, there are secondary limits. For example, you must have earned income (income reported on Form W-2 or Form 1099). Passive (unearned) income does not count – including capital gains, dividends, bond coupons, interest, AND rental income (unless you have a rental property company that files a corporate return and pays you income as a pass-through). However, a change from 2019 permits contributions to continue past age 70½ provided that there is earned income. In addition, depending on a host of other factors, including total income, tax-filing status, participation in another tax qualified plan by you or your spouse, contributions to a Roth IRA, etc., some or even all of the contributions to a traditional IRA may be not tax-deductible.

There are no limits on how much can be rolled over into a traditional IRA. In fact, when an employee retires, it is common advice to roll the 401(k) into a traditional IRA. Doing so removes limitations on investment choices that exist in most 401(k) plans, may substantially lower costs and generally improves overall individual choice and control. There are limited circumstances where a roll-over is not recommended, but more often than not, doing so can provide overall benefit.

Self-Directed IRA - A self-directed IRA differs from a traditional IRA predominantly in what the IRA may use as its underlying investment. Traditional IRAs are built upon traditional investments: mutual funds, individual stocks, bonds, exchange-traded funds (ETFs), annuities, bank accounts, etc. What is common among all these underlying investment classes is that they are held by a third party custodian for the benefit of the individual IRA owner but are otherwise kept at "arm's length" from that individual.

In a self-directed IRA, the permissible asset classes are broader. In addition to allowable assets in traditional IRAs, self-directed plans may include real estate (actual and real estate trusts), precious metals, promissory notes, private placement securities, etc. There are certain assets that are not allowed. For example: collectables (antiques, art, coins, sports memorabilia, stamps, etc.), or any property owned directly (i.e., NOT held by a third party). However, along with this broadened investment choice menu is an enhanced set of rules, and failure to be very familiar with, and follow them all can get an individual in a lot of trouble:

- **The Prohibited Transaction Rule** – This places restrictions on who can contribute and what can be contributed, including additional restrictions such as a moratorium on a self-directed IRA applying for a credit card.

- **Contribution and RMD Rules** – There are certain rules about how and when both contributions and RMDs may be made.

- **Tax Obligations** – While mostly this is identical to other IRAs, including tax deferral, there are two specific cases where taxes may be reported annually: Unrelated business income tax and unrelated debt finance income.

- **Reporting Requirements** – Unlike traditional IRAs, there may be up to three additional tax filings which may be required from a self-directed IRA: Forms 4948, 1099R and 990T.

Anyone contemplating the establishment of a self-directed IRA is strongly encouraged to first seek professional tax advice from a licensed CPA or tax attorney.

Spousal IRA – This plan allows a working spouse to contribute to a non-working spouse's IRA. As such, it offers an exception to the rule that an individual must have earned income to contribute. There are limits based on both total earned income and the existence of other IRA or qualified plans. Anyone contemplating the use of a spousal IRA is encouraged to seek professional tax advice from a licensed CPA or tax attorney.

Inherited IRA – When the owner of an IRA dies, IRS rules mandate that the IRA is liquidated (and taxes paid). Prior to the SECURE Act, there were allowances for an inherited IRA to "Stretch" meaning be liquidated over a beneficiary's lifetime. Presently, with few exceptions, an inherited IRA must be fully liquidated within 10 years of the year in which the IRA owner died.

Spousal Beneficiary – When an IRA is inherited by a legal spouse, that person is afforded exclusive benefits. A spouse beneficiary may:

- Combine the inherited IRA with his/her own and proceed with deferral (if not personally at the required beginning age) or RMDs at his/her own age or the age of deceased spouse, whoever is younger.

- Liquidate the IRA without incurring the 10% tax penalty, even if younger than age 59½ (ordinary income tax liability still exists).

Non-Spouse Beneficiary – With limited exception, anyone other than a legal spouse who inherits an IRA must begin liquidation no later than the year after the year of death. The inherited IRA may NOT be combined with that individual's own IRA and that beneficiary may NOT defer RMDs until the RBA. See more in Chapter 10: Inheriting IRAs.

Non-Taxable IRAs

There are times when an individual may contribute to an IRA on an after-tax basis. When this occurs, the principal may be received without being taxed (taxes were already paid). However, any growth is taxed as ordinary income (exactly like principal and growth in a Traditional IRA). From a tax standpoint, non-taxable IRAs work like non-IRA annuities where in the deposit is untaxed upon receipt but because the growth was tax-deferred, it is taxed as ordinary income to either the owner or a beneficiary.

RMDs and Tax Brackets

There is a significant difference between income that is "taxable" and income that is actually "taxed." To understand this fundamental difference, let's take a quick look at Form 1040. NOTE: Form 1040 underwent substantial changes in 2018 from previous years, among which was considerable simplification of the tax filing form.

Despite a lot of common "noise" about how complex our tax system is, at the most basic level, income tax determination is very simple. Form 1040 (the income tax filing form) has two parts.

Part 1 is used to determine how much income is taxable meaning potentially subject to income tax. A tax filer adds all relevant income to arrive at the Adjusted Gross Income (AGI) on Line 7.

Part 2 (Lines 8-15) is used to determine how much is deducted away from the taxable income (AGI) which then determines the actual amount of income that is taxed. The rest (Lines 16-23) determine how much tax you owe (that wasn't already paid). Our current system is a graduated system, meaning there are steps of different levels of tax exposure.

For example, Bill and Susan earn $100,000 per year and they file jointly. In 2020 (for the 2019 tax year) they will owe 10% on the first $19,750, then 12% on income above $19,750 up to $80,250, then 22% above $80,250 to $171,500. However, Bill and Susan get to take a standard deduction of $24,800 (in 2020) so while their Adjusted Gross Income is $100,000, only $75,200 is taxed. Of that, the first $19,750 is taxed at 10% or $1975 and the balance of $55,450 is taxed at 12% ($75,200 − $19,750 = $55,450 X .12 = $6,654). Bill and Susan's total income tax is $8,629 or 8.63% of their total income.

The key is not how much taxable income (AGI) gets reported but the difference between AGI and deductions. As long as deductions equal or exceed taxable income, no income tax is due. That includes distributions from qualified plans even though the money was contributed untaxed.

Assume John and Mary are retired. They receive $40,000 from Social Security and $12,000 in RMDs. That's all the income they have and all they report. Under this circumstance, none of the Social Security is included in the AGI (see CHAPTER 5: Understanding Social Security Taxation) so the only taxable income is the RMD. But John and Mary have a $24,800 standard deduction (2020) which is more than their AGI (taxable income) so they pay $0 income tax. Thus, none of the $12,000 John and Mary withdrew from their IRA is taxed.

Financial planning clients constantly ask for "tricks" to avoid paying income tax on IRA distributions. Honestly, there are no "tricks." The secret is in structuring income (as much as legally possible) to offset AGI by deductions. This simply requires good long-term planning and a willingness to accept that, depending on individual circumstances, it may not be possible.

Roth IRA - Named after Senator William Roth and established by the Taxpayer Relief Act of 1997, these are qualified plans funded with after-tax dollars. They grow not tax-deferred but tax-exempt. The fundamental difference between tax-deferred and tax-exempt is that tax-deferred means not taxed *yet* and tax-exempt means not taxed *ever*.

There are, however, a few rules. First, a person's income cannot be above certain thresholds or they are not permitted to make contributions to a Roth IRA. As of 2020, a single filer cannot contribute to a Roth IRA if his or her income (AGI) is above $139,000 and if it is between $124,000 and $138,999 the maximum allowable contribution is reduced. A couple filing jointly (or qualifying widow/widower) cannot contribute if income is more than $206,000 and contribution limits are reduced if income is between $196,000 and $205,999. The maximum a person may contribute (2020) is $6,000 per person per year plus a $1,000 "catch up" if age 50 or older. The maximum allowable contributions are also limited by earned income. Earned income is that income derived from work. Things like rent from Real Estate, dividends, etc. do not count. Without earned income, no Roth IRA contributions are permitted. With earned income (reported on Forms W-2 or 1099) – even part-time, a person may contribute to a Roth IRA to the lesser of 100% of that income or the annual threshold limits.

A depositor may withdraw principal at any time for any reason, but growth may not be withdrawn in the first five years or before age 59½ whichever comes second. Doing so may result in a 10% tax penalty.

Qualified Longevity Annuity Contract (QLAC) – Created in 2014, this specialized account currently (2020) permits an IRA owner to "shelter" the lesser of 25% or $135,000 of an IRA from RMDs until age 85. The IRA must be transferred into a designated QLAC offered by one of a very limited number of insurance companies. Other accounts including annuities cannot be re-characterized as QLACs after-the-fact. The advantage of course is that from age 72 through age 85, RMDs are deferred. However, at age 85, the RMDs do return and the liquidation rate is greater than what it would have been at age 72. The biggest downside with QLACs is that, at least as of the time of writing, carriers that offer them regard them as mere holding vehicles meaning they offer no growth. So in effect, putting your money in a QLAC is the same as putting the money in a mattress – just to save on the RMDs. Most people would agree the trade-off is not worth the advantage.

IRA is Tax Code, Not an Investment

There is a lot of common confusion about what an IRA is and is not. When financial planners ask clients about what their investments are, they are commonly told "I have an IRA" as though the IRA is a type of investment. It's not. The term IRA refers only to tax code including the tax treatment that account receives in deferral and upon liquidation.

Virtually anything can be an IRA – or NOT an IRA:

- A portfolio of individual stocks can be an IRA – and the exact same portfolio can be NOT an IRA
- A mutual fund can be an IRA, or not an IRA
- An exchange traded fund (ETF) can be an IRA, or not an IRA
- A bond can be an IRA, or not an IRA
- A bank savings account can be an IRA, or not an IRA
- A CD can be an IRA, or not an IRA
- An annuity can be an IRA, or not an IRA
- A real estate trust can be an IRA, or not an IRA
- etc.

A better list would be what CANNOT be an IRA:

- A rare coin collection CANNOT be an IRA
- Collectables, antiques, works of art, etc. CANNOT be an IRA

- Real estate if deeded directly to you CANNOT be an IRA (real estate in a self-directed IRA must be owned indirectly through a third-party custodian or trust administrator).

- Life insurance CANNOT be an IRA (why would anyone want to?)

- Anything that you own and have direct access to that is not held at arm's length by a third party custodian, CANNOT be an IRA.

When it comes time to take RMDs, they are calculated on each and every account. If you have multiple IRA accounts, as long as they are all the same kind of IRA and as long as the correct amounts are taken, the IRS does not care which account the RMDs are drawn from. For example: suppose you have three IRAs, each worth $100,000. At age 72, the total RMD (new table) due is $10,989 ($3,663 each times 3). However, if all three accounts are all traditional IRA, the total may be taken from one, two or three in any combination so long as the total amount taken is not less than $10,989. However, if the three accounts were all different – say one an IRA, one a 401(k) and one a 403(b), each plan must distribute not less than $3,663. Even if you take $10,989 or more from one, you still must take at least $3,663 from each of the other two. Keep in mind that it's a required MINIMUM distribution meaning you may take more, just not less.

Finally, RMDs cannot be made by "rolling" some of the money from IRA to non-IRA. The distribution must literally be paid out to you and reported as taxable income. What you do with that after is up to you – except you must report the distribution as income and potentially pay taxes at whatever tax bracket is applicable. For you to make the RMD, you must liquidate the account to cash, then purchase new shares of the preferred investment. However, suppose you own a fund that is closed to new investors – and that fund holds only qualified (IRA) money. In this case, unless you can take RMDs from another fund, you will forfeit shares in that fund. As soon as you liquidate the shares, whether as RMD or to merely convert from IRA to non-IRA, you have sold the shares and to repurchase means acquiring new shares which are unavailable.

Chapter 4

ROTH IRAS

E stablished by the Taxpayer Relief Act of 1997, a Roth IRA is the only type of qualified account that is income tax exempt. There is a substantial difference between tax-deferred and tax-exempt.

> ***Tax-deferred means not taxed YET.***
> ***Tax exempt means not taxed EVER.***

Roth IRAs are NEVER taxed – well almost never.

Anyone with earned income (remember that means wages reported on Forms W-2 or 1099), may contribute to a Roth IRA provided they don't earn too much money. The contribution limits (2020) are:

Cannot contribute to a Roth if earn more than:

- $139,000 as single filer
- $206,000 as joint filer

May contribute but at reduced limits (phase-outs) if earn:

- $124,000 to $138,999 as single filer
- $196,000 to $205,999 as joint filer

Anyone (2020) earning less than the initial Phase Out levels may contribute up to $6,000 per year (or 100% of their earned income, whichever comes first). People age 50 and older may contribute up to $7,000 per year. Roth contributions cannot be made for a person other than the income earner, or income earner's spouse, and cannot be made if there is no earned income.

Once established, the Roth IRA account grows income tax exempt and remains income tax exempt to anyone who receives the money, whether the Roth IRA owner or the owner's beneficiaries. While the Roth IRA contributions may be withdrawn, tax and penalty-free at any time, the growth cannot be withdrawn sooner than 5 years from the opening of the Roth IRA or by a person younger than 59½, whichever comes second. Premature withdrawal can subject the Roth to a 10% Tax Penalty. That's the "almost never" part.

Unlike all other forms of qualified money (IRA, etc.), Roth IRAs have no required minimum distribution schedule *to the Roth IRA owner*. However, inherited Roth IRAs to anyone other than a spouse have the same mandatory rules of liquidation as inherited traditional IRAs. The only difference between the two is where inherited IRAs are fully taxable, inherited Roth IRAs are not.

There is, however, a bit of a "tax trap" affiliated with inheriting a Roth IRA. Once a Roth is converted, it changes from a tax-advantaged plan to an account with no tax benefits. It doesn't matter that nothing changed in the underlying investments; only the Roth classification was eliminated. And from that point on, gains are taxable exactly the same as any other non-IRA account. The benefit of tax-exempt growth is lost. And, as with the IRA example, if the underlying investment is closed to new investors, as soon as the Roth is liquidated, continued access to that investment is lost.

Roth Conversions

Prior to 2010, a person who earned not more than $100,000 could convert an existing IRA to a Roth IRA even if that person had no earned income. From 2010 and beyond, the $100,000 ceiling was lifted meaning anyone of any net worth can make the conversion. So it begs the question: Is converting a traditional IRA to a Roth IRA a good idea? And the answer is "It depends."

Two Hypothetical Examples:

1. Tom (72) and Ann (70) are retired. They receive $40,000 in combined Social Security benefits. Tom has a pension that pays $12,000 and a 401(k) worth $212,000 that paid $8,000 in RMDs. Tom should NOT convert his 401(k) to a Roth. Without conversion, Tom and Ann include only $4,000 of their Social Security income in their adjusted gross income which, when added to the pension and RMDs is $24,000. After subtracting their $24,800 standard deduction, the amount of income tax owed is $0 and the RMD is received tax-free. But if Tom converted any his 401(k) to Roth, he would owe income tax on that conversion and potentially owe income tax on the Social Security benefit. If Tom converted the entire account in lump sum, 85% of his Social Security would be taxable plus much of the converted 401(k) would be taxed at 24%.

2. Ed and Mary (both 65) report income of $145,000 per year. They also have an IRA worth $850,000, growing at 6% per year. Five years later when, Ed and Mary retire, they will receive $60,000 in combined Social Security benefits but they need more income than that to sustain their lifestyle. Ed and Mary SHOULD convert their IRA to Roth but do so incrementally over the next five years

before starting Social Security. Doing so will cause them to bump from the 22% to 24% top marginal tax bracket but only on a fraction (about 15%) of their converted money. In other words, 2% per year tax increase on 15% of their total income and the rest is taxed at the same rate. Then at age 70, Ed and Mary start Social Security and supplement it with income from their Roth IRA. They can generate a tax-free retirement income of more than $100,000 per year for the rest of their lives.

Some Roth Conversion Guidelines

1. Common claim: "*By converting the IRA to a Roth IRA, I'll grow and compound the money tax-exempt so I'll get more after-tax money later.*" This is mathematically FALSE!

   Within mathematics, there is a law known as the Commutative Property which states that the sequence of multiplicative operations has no effect on the result. In simple terms, here's an example of what that means.

   Let's assume you have a traditional IRA worth $100,000 and are taxed at a flat rate of 25% (just to keep the math simple). If you do NOT convert your IRA and grow it at 6% for 12 years (by the Rule of 72) you will double the money to $200,000. But then you completely liquidate the IRA. You'll pay 25% tax and afterward, you'll have $150,000 tax-free. Now suppose you convert to Roth and pay tax at 25%. Your Roth will open with $75,000. After 12 years at 6% it doubles to $150,000 which is tax-free. There is NO difference.

2. You expect tax rates in the future to be higher. This MIGHT be a good reason to convert but be careful. Remember, the tax structure is graduated meaning there are brackets or "stair-steps" of increasingly higher tax rates. Suppose, for

example, you are near the top of the 12% federal income tax bracket. Converting that hypothetical $100,000 IRA would mean most of it is taxed at the next highest bracket (22%). Conversely, if by not converting and taking RMDs, you remain at the 12% bracket. Then, if the tax rate increases from 12% to 15%, and most of your RMDs are taxed at 15%, you're still saving taxes by NOT converting.

On the other hand, if you are at or slightly above the top of a marginal tax bracket and you can manage the conversions to not bump into the next highest bracket, you suffer no added tax liability for the conversion. Then, if future tax rates rise, you are benefitted.

The lesson to be learned here is that even if you expect tax rates to increase, the value of making the conversion DEPENDS on your individual circumstances

3. Conversion before starting Social Security benefits. This is one of the strongest justifications for making the conversion. As previously demonstrated, the amount of Social Security that is taxable depends primarily on "other reportable income." Generating supplemental income from a Roth as opposed to a traditional IRA can make an enormous difference in how much income is taxed. As we saw with the Ed and Mary example above, strategically making the conversion before starting Social Security provided a substantial tax-free benefit for life in retirement.

4. Inheritance desires. If an IRA (including RMDs) is not needed for personal income and the primary intention for the IRA is inheritance, then making the Roth conversion could be very beneficial to the heirs, provided they will need the money within 10 years of the date of inheritance. Remember: A Roth IRA does not have a distribution

requirement to the owner but to heirs (other than a spouse), it does.

5. Medical needs. If you regard your IRA as a possible source of money to pay for major medical expense, including long term care, making the conversion could be highly beneficial. Withdrawing large sums from an IRA to pay custodial care-givers or uninsured medical expenses, could add insult to injury because the money taken is still taxable and while there may be some opportunity for deductions, most people will find that advantage of minimal value at best. Conversely, taking the money from a Roth IRA incurs no tax exposure and does not add a calamity on top of a tragedy.

6. You do not have to make the conversion all at once. If you determine converting an IRA to Roth IRA is a good idea in general, then as previously illustrated, give consideration to your tax brackets and (like Ed and Mary) strategically convert to minimize the tax bump. But don't simply assume that standard marginal brackets are the only concern. A parallel version of income tax calculation, called the Alternative Minimum Tax (AMT), if triggered can result in a significant increase in tax due. Before deciding to convert, especially if a large IRA, consult with a CPA or other tax professional who is equipped to determine if the conversion would trigger AMT.

7. You cannot undo the conversion. The 2017 Tax Cuts and Jobs Act (TCJA) ended the opportunity for someone who made a Roth conversion to change their minds. If you make the conversion, then realize it was a mistake, you cannot reverse that decision. This is why it is so important to know if making the conversion truly is the best strategy for you.

The decision to convert or not convert is one that requires consideration of a host of variables in light of larger planning questions. It is not a simple "black or white" ("good or bad") strategy. For some people, converting could be a highly advantageous; for others, it could be detrimental.

Chapter 5

UNDERSTANDING SOCIAL SECURITY TAXATION

W hy is there a chapter about Social Security Taxation in a book about IRAs? It's because the two form a significant bulk of retirement income and many people incorrectly plan when and how to access them. Doing so may result in less retirement income and paying more taxes on what you do get.

Unfortunately, there are a number of commonly espoused misstatements about Social Security, including how it is taxed.

For example, a popular notion is that if a couple earns more than $32,000, then fifty percent (50%) of their Social Security income will be taxed. And if they earn more than $44,000, then eighty five percent (85%) will be taxed. For single filers, this line of thought assumes an income of $25,000 for 50% exposure and $34,000 for 85% exposure. In a word, nonsense! For illustrative purposes, we'll focus on couples who file jointly.

To calculate how much Social Security income is reported as taxable income (meaning added to the AGI), the IRS provides an 18-step calculation. This worksheet asks the tax-filer (thrice) to make two parallel calculations and take the lesser of the two. In addition, the figure "$44,000" never directly occurs on the worksheet. Rather that value is improperly derived from the sum of two separate values ($32,000 and $12,000), both of which are used as income reducers and are instructed separately because their application is different in later steps on the worksheet.

The easiest way to see this is simply to look at the Social Security Benefits Worksheet supplied in the official instructions for completing Form 1040 (see page 51).

Line 1 asks you to list your total Social Security benefit.

Lines 2-7 are used to sum an income value from which subtractions and reductions are made.

It starts with one half the Social Security benefit (Line 2), added to the sum of all other countable income (Lines 3-5), less certain allowable above-the-line deductions (Line 6) to arrive at a final sum (Line 7). If Line 7 is $0 or less, the instruction says "*STOP. None of your social security benefits are taxable.*" If the subtraction of Line 6 from Line 5 is greater than $0, then you continue.

Line 8 then instructs: "*If you are Married filing jointly, enter $32,000.*"

Line 9 instructs: subtract that from Line 7. If the result is $0 or less, the instructions say "*STOP. None of your social security benefits are taxable.*"

But if you must keep going, then

Social Security Benefits Worksheet—Lines 5a and 5b *Keep for Your Records*

Before you begin:
- Figure any write-in adjustments to be entered on the dotted line next to Schedule 1, line 36 (see the instructions for Schedule 1, line 36).
- If you are married filing separately and you lived apart from your spouse for all of 2018, enter "D" to the right of the word "benefits" on line 5a. If you don't, you may get a math error notice from the IRS.
- Be sure you have read the *Exception* in the line 5a and 5b instructions to see if you can use this worksheet instead of a publication to find out if any of your benefits are taxable.

1. Enter the total amount from **box 5** of **all** your **Forms SSA-1099** and **Forms RRB-1099.** Also, enter this amount on Form 1040, line 5a ..... 1. _____

2. Multiply line 1 by 50% (0.50) .... 2. _____

3. Combine the amounts from Form 1040, lines 1, 2b, 3b, 4b, and Schedule 1, line 22 .... 3. _____

4. Enter the amount, if any, from Form 1040, line 2a .... 4. _____

5. Combine lines 2, 3, and 4 .... 5. _____

6. Enter the total of the amounts from Schedule 1, lines 23 through 32, plus any write-in adjustments you entered on the dotted line next to Schedule 1, line 36 other than any amounts identified as "DPAD" .... 6. _____

7. Is the amount on line 6 less than the amount on line 5?
   - ☐ **No. STOP** None of your social security benefits are taxable. Enter -0- on Form 1040, line 5b.
   - ☐ **Yes.** Subtract line 6 from line 5 .... 7. _____

8. If you are:
   - Married filing jointly, enter $32,000
   - Single, head of household, qualifying widow(er), or married filing separately and you **lived apart** from your spouse for all of 2018, enter $25,000
   - Married filing separately and you lived with your spouse at any time in 2018, skip lines 8 through 15; multiply line 7 by 85% (0.85) and enter the result on line 16. Then, go to line 17
   .... 8. _____

9. Is the amount on line 8 less than the amount on line 7?
   - ☐ **No. STOP** None of your social security benefits are taxable. Enter -0- on Form 1040, line 5b. If you are married filing separately and you **lived apart** from your spouse for all of 2018, be sure you entered "D" to the right of the word "benefits" on line 5a.
   - ☐ **Yes.** Subtract line 8 from line 7 .... 9. _____

10. Enter: $12,000 if married filing jointly; $9,000 if single, head of household, qualifying widow(er), or married filing separately and you **lived apart** from your spouse for all of 2018 .... 10. _____

11. Subtract line 10 from line 9. If zero or less, enter -0- .... 11. _____

12. Enter the **smaller** of line 9 or line 10 .... 12. _____

13. Enter one-half of line 12 .... 13. _____

14. Enter the **smaller** of line 2 or line 13 .... 14. _____

15. Multiply line 11 by 85% (0.85). If line 11 is zero, enter -0- .... 15. _____

16. Add lines 14 and 15 .... 16. _____

17. Multiply line 1 by 85% (0.85) .... 17. _____

18. **Taxable social security benefits.** Enter the **smaller** of line 16 or line 17. Also enter this amount on Form 1040, line 5b .... 18. _____

TIP *If any of your benefits are taxable for 2018 **and** they include a lump-sum benefit payment that was for an earlier year, you may be able to reduce the taxable amount. See Lump-Sum Election in Pub. 915 for details.*

Line 10 instructs: "*Enter $12,000.*"

Line 11 instructs: "*Subtract Line 10 from Line 9.*"

Line 12 instructs: "*Enter the **smaller** of Line 9 or Line 10.*" The word "*smaller*" is written in bold face.

Line 13 instructs: divide Line 12 in half.

Line 14 instructs: "*Enter the **smaller** of line 2 or Line 13*". The word "smaller" is in bold face. Line 2 represents **half** of the total Social Security income.

Line 15 instructs: "*Multiply Line 11 by 85% (0.85)*." This is the first time 85% is even mentioned but it does not mean 85% of the total Social Security benefit is taxable. That's because Line 11 represents a value that includes half the total Social Security benefit, less the sum of $32,000 and $12,000 (hence the $44,000).

Line 16 instructs: "*Add lines 14 and 15.*" Both these lines represent reduced values from actual.

Line 17 instructs: "*Multiply Line 1 by 85% (0.85)*." Now, for the first time does the specter of 85% of Social Security being taxed occur. But then...

Line 18 instructs: "*Enter the **smaller** of line 16 or line 17*." This is the amount of Social Security that is actually reported as taxable.

In other words, unless you have so much income that after all the subtractions, and divisions by two, and taking the lesser of two amounts (three times), the result (Line 16) is still greater than 85% of your total Social Security benefit, then (and only then) is 85% of your Social Security actually taxable.

Thus, as we can see, whether or not Social Security income is taxed depends entirely on the amount of "other income" that is reported.

For example: Let's assume Jim and Sally receive $64,000 of combined Social Security and no other reportable, taxable income. According to the "traditional" theory, 85% of that income will be taxed. However, the correct amount Social Security Income reported as taxable is $0:

Line 1. Enter total Social Security income = $64,000

Line 2. Multiply Line 1 by 50% = $32,000

Lines 3-4. List all other income sources = $0

Line 5. Add Lines 2, 3, 4 = $32,000

Line 6. List all above-the-line deductions = $0

Line 7. Subtract Line 6 from Line 5 = $32,000

Line 8. Enter $32,000

Line 9. Subtract Line 8 from Line 7: $32,000 – $32,000 = $0.

"*STOP. None of your social security benefits are taxable.*"

Now let's take this a step further. Assume Jim and Sally's combined Social Security income is $88,000 (technically not possible but let's assume it to illustrate the point) and that's all the reportable income they have.

Lines 1-7. Half Social Security plus all other income = $44,000

Line 9. Subtract $32,000 = $12,000

Line 10. Enter $12,000 = $12,000

Line 11. Line 9 minus Line 10 = $0

Line 13. Half of the **smaller** of Line 9 or 10 = $6,000

Line 14. **Smaller** of Line 2 or Line 13 = $6,000

Line 15. Line 11 X 85%) = $0

Line 16. Add Lines 14 and 15 = $6,000

Line 17. Multiply Line 1 (total Social Security) by 85% = $74,800

Line 18. Enter the **smaller** of Line 16 or 17 on Form 1040 = $6,000

Therefore, $6,000 of the Social Security is reported as taxable (AGI). Since there is no other income, the AGI is $6,000. Now subtract standard deduction ($24,800) and NONE of the Social Security is taxed.

Now let's assume Jim and Sally receive $28,000 in Social Security benefits plus $60,000 from other (taxable) sources.

Their gross income is the same $88,000 as before but the tax picture changes dramatically:

Line 7. Half of Social Security plus all other income = $74,000

Line 9. Subtract $32,000 = $47,000

Line 10. Enter $12,000 = $12,000

Line 11. Line 9 minus Line 10 = $30,000

Line 12. Smaller of Line 9 or Line 10 = $12,000

Line 13. Half of Line 12 = $6,000

Line 14. Smaller of Line 2 or Line 13 = $6,000

Line 15. Line 11 × 85% = $25,500

Line 16. Add Lines 14 and 15 = $31,500

Line 17. Multiply Line 1 by 85% = $23,800

Line 18. Smaller of Line 16 or Line 17 = $23,800

Their AGI is now $83,800 ($23,800 from Social Security + $60,000 from "Other Income"). Subtract $24,800 (standard deduction) and Jim and Sally will pay income tax on $59,000.

What just happened? Two identical total incomes ($88,000), one composed entirely of Social Security and the other mostly not. In the former case, NONE of the Social Security is taxed and NONE of the total income is taxed. In the latter case 85% of the Social Security and over 95% of the total income is taxed.

This is why the amount of Social Security income that may be taxed is entirely dependent on the "other income." Moreover, there is no such thing as a finite 50% vs. 85% pivot. The actual amount varies continuously from 0% to 85% largely depending on "Other Income."

"Other Income" can be characterized in two ways: Income that is changeable and income that is not. Income that is NOT changeable includes RMDs, pensions, etc. - things that once established, cannot be easily undone. Conversely, some income comes from things that occur by choice and can be changed. Strategically doing so can offer a significant impact on the amount of Social Security (and other) income that ultimately gets taxed. Some of the more common forms of changeable "other income" are dividends (especially if reinvested), investment portfolio turn-over (buying and selling by you or a fund manager), interest and bond coupon payments (including municipal bonds!)

Sound retirement income planning requires a consideration of ALL income sources in combination with the Social Security income amounts. Then strategies are developed to decrease tax exposure, where possible, without reducing total income (which would defeat the purpose). This is precisely where IRA distribution strategies offer potential tax savings.

What is surprising to many is that many traditional "tax-free" or tax-advantaged sources municipal bond and qualified dividend income) COUNT toward the taxability of Social Security. Anyone who receives or soon will receive Social Security benefits should give pause to a financial adviser who says "such and such" generates tax-free income. That may not be entirely true. A few things (e.g., Roth IRA) don't count, but most "non-taxable" income sources count.

Chapter 6

STATE INCOME TAX LOADS

Depending on the state you live in, withdrawals from IRAs may or may not be taxed as income. As of 2020, 23 states do not tax some or any of a filer's tax retirement benefits, but the rules and circumstances differ. The following is a summary of those tax-favored states. However, it is important to understand that even within a single state, tax exemptions may vary, and these provisions are current only as of the time of writing. Changes to future state tax law are possible and those changes, if they occur, may increase or decrease the opportunities.

Seven states have no state income tax at all: Alaska, Florida, Nevada, South Dakota, Texas, Washington, Wyoming and Tennessee. Two others, New Hampshire and Tennessee do not tax wages.

All the remaining states do impose state income tax but 16 offer limited non-taxable benefits on retirement income:

Alabama: Does not tax income from defined benefit plans (pensions). However, withdrawals from other qualified plans (401(k) and IRA) ARE included for the state's income tax.

Arkansas: If you are retired and drawing retirement benefits, the first $6,000 of income from employer-sponsored pension plans qualify for a $6,000 exclusion. This exclusion also applies to distributions from traditional IRAs received after age 59½. In addition, certain Arkansas residents who participated in either the McFadden or Maples v. Weiss lawsuits may be eligible for additional benefits.

Delaware: For persons 60 and older, up to $12,500 may be excluded from state income tax on dividends, capital gains, interest, rental income and distributions from qualified plans. Persons under age 60, $2,000 is exempt.

Georgia: For persons 65 and older, up to $65,000 of "retirement income" is exempted and up to $35,000 for persons 62 to 64. "retirement income" may include distributions from qualified plans, pensions and annuities as well as a suite of other income sources.

Hawaii: Income from defined benefit plans (pensions) is state tax exempt. In some cases, income from defined contribution plans (401(k), etc.) may also qualify as state income tax exempt.

Illinois: Income from any qualified retirement plan is not taxed.

Iowa: For persons 55 and older, up to $6,000 of benefits from a qualified plan or annuity are excluded. Additional benefits exist including reduced tax exposure on Social Security benefits.

Kentucky: Up to $41,110 of income from pensions, IRAs, annuities, profit-sharing plans are state tax exempt. However, the exclusion amount is not subject to an annual inflation adjustment.

Louisiana: For persons 65 and older, up to $6,000 of pension and annuity income plus certain other income sources may be excluded.

Michigan: For persons born before 1946, up to $49,861 in pension and retirement income is excluded. Some additional restrictions and opportunities do exist.

Mississippi: For persons 59½ and older, income from any qualified plan is state income tax exempt.

New York: For persons 59½ and older, up to $20,000 of pension, IRA and annuity income is exempt.

North Carolina: Certain government employees who qualify under the Bailey Act (Bailey v. State of North Carolina) may receive qualified plan benefits (State 401(k) and 457 plans) free from state income tax provided the income comes directly from those designated plans. Rolling a Bailey-qualified plan to another qualified plan invalidates the tax exemption.

Pennsylvania: For residents 60 and older, in most cases, qualified retirement plan income is state tax-exempt.

South Carolina: For persons 65 and older, up to $10,000 of any income, (except Social Security) is taxed. However, up to $15,000 of retirement income may be exempted depending on specific criteria.

In addition, only 13 states tax Social Security benefits: Colorado, Connecticut, Kansas, Minnesota, Missouri, Montana, Nebraska, New Mexico, North Dakota, Rhode Island, Utah, Vermont, and West Virginia. The rest do not.

As can be seen, taxation rules can differ dramatically state by state. The summaries noted above are just that: summaries. This is why it is important to consult a CPA or other licensed tax-planning professional *in your state*. Often, when people move, they keep the tax planner they used previously. Loyalty is a great thing but a CPA from one state may not be entirely up to speed on the tax nuances in another. In such circumstances, there could be a cost for that loyalty in the form of missing out on tax-savings opportunities that are esoteric to the new state of residence. Rule of thumb: When you change your state of residence, change your financial and tax planning advisors.

Chapter 7

RMDS VS SOCIAL SECURITY – TIMING/TAXATION

During your working years, you pay for tomorrow by what you do today. When you retire, you pay for tomorrow by what you did yesterday.

R etirees, faced with the fear of outliving their money, often make knee-jerk decisions that are not necessarily in their best interest. In other words, they panic. They look around at their options and there is Social Security – beckoning to them. Intuitively, many retirees know that delaying Social Security increases the total benefit but not knowing how much. Unnecessarily worried about an imminent demise of Social Security, they trigger their benefits. In addition, they also look at their 401(k) or IRA and reject the notion of spending any of it. Common justifications are: The taxes are terrible, I don't want to spend it away, it's for my kids, etc.

Unfortunately, all these common reactions serve to lead the retiree down a path that may not in their long-term best interest.

Some basic facts:

1. Once you pay into Social Security and qualify for benefits (after ten years), those benefits CANNOT be taken away.

2. Social Security benefits are NEVER 100% taxable. At worst, 15% of your Social Security income is not taxed. At best, none of it is and as we've already seen, that depends on what your "other income" is.

3. Social Security benefits grow by ⅔% per month (8% per year) starting from age 62 and continuing through age 70 *if you wait* before electing benefits. Then, after you start, your Social Security income is increased by inflation. There are very few retirement income programs with any index to inflation, but Social Security is one.

4. Your IRA, 401(k), etc. is almost always 100% taxable, must be liquidated and you cannot change those things. Because of taxability, they also do not inherit well. They were specifically designed to be *your* retirement income and not using them for that purpose is to reject the reason for which they were designed.

For example, Bob & Mary, both 65 have just retired. Together, they receive a pension of $1,300 per month and are eligible (at 65) for Social Security benefits totaling $3700 month. They need $5,000 per month to live. They also have 401(k) accounts totaling $300,000.

Succumbing to the "conventional wisdom" myths and seeing no other way out, Bob and Mary "bite the bullet" and start their Social Security income, justifying that "at least it's enough." Over the next five years, they are also pleased that the 401(k) continues to grow at 6% per year. Seven years later, it's worth $451,089 and will generate a required minimum distribution of $15,442 ($1,287 per month). Let's assume no inflation so their regular income and need are still $5,000 per month ($60,000 per year). Now their total income is $75,442. Even better is that only $13,856 of their Social Security is reported as taxable. Their adjusted gross income is $44,898. Bob and Mary are happy.

But if they did it right and withdrew $3,700 per month from the 401(k), until age 70 ($210,000 withdrawn over five years), the 401(k) will be worth $151,180. Now, Social Security income will have increased to $58,800 and they can stop withdrawing from the 401(k). Their income from Social Security plus Pension is now $74,400 for which their tax bill for the text two years will be $0. Over that time, the 401(k) continues to grow (presumably 6% per year). By age 72, it will be worth $169,867 and their first year RMD will be $5807. Their new gross income is now $80,207 of which only $8393 is taxed (assuming 2020 standard deduction).

Bob and Mary then benefit from one additional aspect. Social Security's cost of living adjustment (COLA) which increases the benefit based on inflation. There are multiple ways to measure inflation but the one widely regarded as the most accurate is the CPI-U (Consumer Price Index for All Urban Measures). This index includes not only the traditional national measures of inflation but also gas prices, groceries and home heating fuel – and that's what Social Security uses to make its annual COLA increases. If Bob and Mary took their Social Security benefits at age 65 ($3,500/month) and there is a 2.5% COLA, the dollar increase will be $87.50/month. If they waited until 70 and got a 2.5% increase on $4,900 (40% total increase for the 5 years), their COLA increase would be \$122.50/month. Even if they compounded with COLA over 5 years (ages 65 to 70), their inflation-adjusted income at 70 would be \$3,959.93 vs. \$4,900. By age 75 with the same COLA, those incomes would be \$4,480.30 vs. \$5,543.90. By waiting, not only did they get more raw income at 70 (\$940.07/month), but the spread increased to \$1,063.60 by age 75. This is advantageous because multiplying a larger base number by a fixed percentage results in a larger product (more money).

Ultimately, Bob and Mary still have some additional considerations before deciding which strategy to use. For example, if their 401(k) is invested in volatile positions, withdrawing \$44,400 per year from an initial investment of \$300,000 (14.8% first year) is very risky. If markets plunge any time during the five years, Bob and Mary might face losing most if not all of their 401(k). Also, depending on what other (non-IRA) assets they own, the decision to spend down the 401(k) may be affected. For example, if they have only that 401(k) and nothing else, then their decision to spend it down might jeopardize their liquidity for future years. Conversely, if they have other, non-qualified accounts, and they're able to transfer the 401(k) into low risk investments, then the risk of spending it down is significantly reduced. Finally, they need to consider issues of inheritance, potential medical expense needs, possible major changes to their future cost of living, etc. Nonetheless, as a general rule, it is advantageous to delay starting Social Security benefits until age 70 unless dire economic circumstances or poor health dictate otherwise.

In addition, retirees who have some money in qualified accounts and some in non-qualified accounts are benefitted by prioritizing which is to be used as retirement income and which is to be grown for discretionary use or inheritance.

Given all other things being equal, the default wisdom is to convert the IRA money into a "personal pension" (generate a lifetime income stream) and grow the non-IRA money. Here's why: The IRA money is required to be liquidated starting at the required beginning age (whether 70½ or 72) and is 100% taxable as ordinary income to anyone – Bob, Mary or their heirs. The non-IRA money, if growth is by capital appreciation not dividends or interest (which are taxable every year as ordinary income whether taken or not), then there is no tax consequence until the money is actually spent. And when it is – if by the account owner or spouse is received at a lower tax rate: long-term capital gain rate. But if inherited, the heirs receive a "step-up in basis" meaning the inherited cost value is the same as on the date of death and if liquidated, incurs NO income tax consequence.

For example, assume Bob and Mary also have $300,000 of non-IRA money (e.g., in a brokerage account). If rather than taking RMDs, they convert the 401(k) into a personal pension and generate lifetime income (estimated $7,500/ year for life) their total income further increases to about $84,300/year. The lifetime income counts as the required minimum distribution (Rule 72-t) for that account. It is fixed and constant, easier to schedule and requires no more adjustments or annual calculation. Bob and Mary can then grow their non-IRA money for future discretionary needs. If they find they have more income than they need, that surplus can be added to the non-IRA account and grow without an IRS withdrawal demand. If they reversed it and generated income from the non-IRA money, not only do they still have a RMD, any surplus income getting added back into the non-IRA account creates a "revolving door" that actually reduces the ability for the account to grow by compounding (think back to our little income game).

Chapter 8

TWO TYPES OF INCOME

If you never spend it, it's inheritance, not income.

For most people, during their working years, income is nothing more than that automatic paycheck which is deposited weekly or bi-weekly. People know it's there, expect it and hardly think much more about it than that. They may also have a retirement account such as a 401(k) that is funded by automatic pay deductions and employer matching. Both are very much "off the radar." Yet, it wasn't that long ago that a paycheck was literally that: a physical check handed out each and every week which must then be taken to the bank and deposited. For a minority of people, that's still true but that group is growing smaller and smaller. Regardless of how an employee got paid, the one constant was that the income was constant. It was expected, counted on and reliable. And that reliability was essential because monthly bills are also expected, counted on and very much reliable – and the consequence for not paying the bills was (is) serious.

"**Required Income**" is defined as that necessary and expected weekly, bi-monthly or monthly paycheck. In other words, required income is precisely that: required. It cannot be subject to volatility or uncertainty and cannot be "hit or miss."

"Lifestyle Income" is really not income as much as a ready source of funds to pay for the non-necessities of life: vacations, recreation, leisure, etc. (Okay so maybe you consider golf or your hair "necessary" but if you miss a golf date, hair appointment, or whatever, etc. you won't lose your house, have utilities disconnected or be referred to collections). Sometimes, Lifestyle Income needs are as regular as required income (golf, hair, etc.) and sometimes it's periodic or occasional (vacations, etc.). It doesn't really matter because it's fundamentally a separate pool of money and is (or should be) regarded separately from the pool that provides the required income.

During working years, particularly if employed by someone other than yourself, the biggest worry about maintaining your required income is simply maintaining your job. If you work, you get paid and that's your required income source. For most people, getting paid more than is necessary to pay the required bills is also the source of their lifestyle income. In this regard at least, life, when working, is easy.

However, everything changes when a person retires.

The difference between employment and retirement is that while employed, today and tomorrow are paid by what you do today and tomorrow. In retirement, today and tomorrow are paid by what you did yesterday.

From the perspective of retirement planning, how the money allocated toward Required Income is managed differently from the money allocated to Lifestyle.

Managing Required Income

As already noted, required income must be risk-free. When you are employed, if you are ever at risk of losing your job, the stress of that can be overwhelming. Why? Because losing your job means the loss of your primary income and that means the inability to pay your bills. Conversely, when your job is secure and not at risk, you feel confident in the knowledge that your primary income will be reliable and that the amount you receive is known. Retirement is no different. This is why the #1 concern among retirees is the possibility of outliving their money.

The original purpose of an IRA (all qualified money really), was to provide income from the date of retirement for the rest of your life. This is the reason that Robert Merton was so critical of corporate America's shift from defined benefit to defined contribution plans. The primary value of a defined benefit plan (pension) is that the primary concern of outliving ones money is alleviated. Unfortunately, with the shift from pensions to 401(k) plans, not only did the risk of future income shift from the employer to the employee, that shift includes no instructions how to convert a bag of money into a permanent income for life.

Nonetheless, the intended purpose of an IRA is to be that source; to supplement Social Security and offer a retiree the means of living comfortably for the rest of his or her life. It is the reason why IRAs are tax-deferred accounts, why there is a mandatory distribution schedule (RMDs) and why the rules of inherited IRAs are more complex and less "friendly" than they are for the original IRA owner. Accordingly, the most logical conclusion from all this is that an IRA (any qualified plan) should be regarded as a primary source of income in retirement. And yes, the income they generate is taxable, but so was employment income so in that regard, it's no different. Of course, when combined with Social Security that is never more than 85% taxable, the combination of those sources is to provide a tax-reduced total required income compared with what it was while employed. And while it is desirable to ensure efficient inheritance transfer of unspent qualified money, that was never its original purpose.

Retirees fall into three broad categories regarding their IRAs as primary retirement income.

1. The RMDs are not needed for retirement living.

2. The RMDs are needed and adequate for retirement.

3. The RMDs are inadequate for retirement and more money is needed.

For retirees fortunate enough to fit the first category, the primary challenge is not so much managing the account for their lives, but managing it for eventual transfer or inheritance. It's ironic that so many people profess they don't want to spend a dime of their IRA, and grow it indefinitely, but have no specific inheritance plan other than "my kids will get it." The biggest problem with this is the tax consequences of an inherited IRA that is not carefully managed. There are multiple strategies for addressing this but failure to address it through at least one avenue is to "pass the buck" on a potential big tax liability to others.

For retirees in the second category, the most important consideration is simply to preserve the account. This is accomplished by ensuring principal protection and having enough reasonable growth to offset account reduction by the schedule of RMDs.

Retirees in the third category will need more aggressive income planning to not only preserve and protect the principal of the account, but also to squeeze as much income as physically possible from whatever has been accumulated.

These are also the people who may have to work longer that desired, to give their account a little more time to grow.

Managing Lifestyle Income

The considerations for Lifestyle Income are completely different than required income. At this point, let's shift the terminology a bit and refer to this as Discretionary Income meaning it is optional.

Taxes – Withdrawing money from a pool of funds for personal leisure should have the least possible tax consequences. For example, suppose a retired couple has $2,500 per month in Social Security and $2,500 per month from IRA distributions. They will be taxed on barely more than 20% of their gross income. If, however, they withdraw $10,000 for a vacation, not only will that increase the tax load on their Social Security, but also increase their total taxable income by virtue of the withdrawal itself. It's a form of double taxation. Conversely, if the $10,000 was withdrawn from a tax-advantaged or tax-free source, it not only reduces their total taxable income but also the tax load on Social Security.

Liquidity - Required income from IRAs does not need to be any more liquid than sufficient to generate the required monthly income. When you were working, you had no access to money from your employer beyond your paycheck. When you get a Pension, you have no greater access to the money than what the Pension pays each month. Required income liquidity need be no greater *provided the IRA is not your only source of money*. But a bucket of money designated as the source of discretionary uses, need be more liquid.

Risk vs. Growth - Because discretionary (non-IRA) money has no short-term requirement to perform (because you don't have to withdraw if you don't want), then accepting some risk in exchange for growth is acceptable. Within the investment community, there is a broad assumption that to increase return, an investor must increase risk. This however, is not true. As far back as 1964 and 1966, Stanford economist William F. Sharpe proposed simple equations to permit risk and return potential to be compared in what was called a risk-adjusted return. His work earned him the Nobel Prize in Economics (for his 1964 Capital Asset Pricing Model). Consider the following example. Suppose you are comparing two different investments, each with identical historical return. But the first has twice the volatility (risk) of the second. Obviously, the second choice is better. So what if the average return on the first was greater than the second but the risk on the second was less than the first? A risk-adjusted return calculation would not only reveal which one was better, but also offer a value as to how much.

The degree of tolerable risk in a discretionary account is going to vary widely depending on both the overall risk tolerance of an individual investor and the relative risk tolerance affiliated with that particular portfolio. For example, consider two investors each with a moderate level of risk tolerance. The first has all his money in risky accounts. The second has only half his money in risky accounts. Adding a risky investment to the total portfolio is more acceptable for the second investor (because he has "room"). Finally is the matter of the relative size of the accounts. Investing $10,000 with a net worth of less than $100,000 is more risky than investing $100,000 with a net worth more than $1 million.

Chapter 9

IRAS AND ANNUITIES

Some Basics

When it comes to this broad category of financial products, a lot of hype and emotionally-charged love/hate hyperbole is commonly flung around, much of which is false. Before proceeding on this discussion, I want to make three very strong statements of fact about annuities from which this chapter will proceed:

1. Annuities are accounts from insurance companies. Nothing less, nothing more. **Period.**

2. There are thousands of different annuities of many different categories from scores of insurance companies, offering a myriad of potential benefits for very different purposes. Other than point number 1, the notion that all annuities are alike, that they offer similar benefits, or have similar expenses and restrictions, etc. is patently false. **Period.**

3. Depending on a person's *specific needs and circumstances*, some annuities may be highly beneficial while others would be entirely inappropriate. It's all about individual circumstances. **Period.**

To summarize:

> **No single annuity is right for everybody and no single annuity is right for anybody's every dollar. Period.**

A Bit of History

Annuities were first invented during the Roman Empire to compensate soldiers for their military service. In fact, the word "annuity" is derived from the Latin "annua" meaning annual payments. During the Middle Ages, they were used similarly by rulers to pay soldiers for their conquests. In 1720, the Presbyterian Church introduced annuities into the American Colonies to provide income for clergy and their families in perpetuities. In 1790, Benjamin Franklin bequeathed annuities to the cities of Philadelphia and Boston. The latter, in the 1990's, after more than 200 years of income finally decided to cash it out. Abraham Lincoln used annuities to compensate wounded Union soldiers and their families. From 1923 through 1929, Babe Ruth contributed more than half his salary to annuities and relied on them through the Great Depression. He famously said "*I may take risks in life, but I will never risk my money. I use annuities and I never have to worry about my money.*"

Yet, there are advisors who hate all annuities on principal. It's because they cannot sell them and therefore don't know much about what it is they cannot sell except that it's the competition (the "enemy"). Conversely, there are advisors who love annuities and hate everything else on principal. It's because annuities are the only thing they *can* sell and therefore don't know much about what it is they cannot sell except it's the competition (the "enemy").

To be blunt: anyone with a blanket "love/hate" attitude

about any category of financial products (including annuities) has their personal best interests ahead of yours. They're NOT fiduciary. Avoid them.

Understanding Annuities

Broadly, annuities can be categorized as fitting into a couple of categories:

Immediate vs. Deferred - An immediate annuity is essentially a pure pension. A sum of money is converted into a guaranteed income for a stated period of time that may be for life of one or two people, for a stated number of years or combinations of both. This is a process known as Annuitization. A Deferred Annuity is an account which is permitted to grow for either a defined or undefined amount of time. In the former case, like a CD, the term may be renewed. In the latter case, there is no requirement to renew, annuitize or otherwise. The money is simply allowed to grow until the owner wants to access it.

Fixed vs. Variable - These terms have nothing to do with growth. Technically, a fixed annuity is one where deposits (called "Premiums") may be comingled with the company's general funds account. A Variable Annuity is one where the premiums must be held in a separate account. In the former case, the issuing company has direct access to the funds to earn for the company. In the latter, they do not so they must charge fees. Functionally, a fixed annuity is a pure insurance contract wherein the issuing company assumes all risk of loss associated with volatile markets. Conversely, a variable annuity is a combination contract that pairs an insurance company with market investments, commonly mutual funds. In these cases, the issuing company transfers the risk associated with markets to the annuity owner although in some cases may offer to sell the owner an insurance policy against loss. The big difference here is that in a fixed annuity, the safety component is part of the standard contract. In a variable annuity it is a rider available for purchase. Other important differences exist.

One of the most significant advantages with deferred annuities (as opposed to immediate) is that annuity growth is tax-deferred. Thus, when money grows inside an annuity, that growth is never taxed until withdrawn. The long-term advantage of tax-deferred growth has already been discussed. Another common advantage with annuities is that, if properly set up, annuities automatically bypass probate including provide, under contract, the potential to direct, by fiduciary contract, not only who receives inherited money but through defined payment schedules including lifetime. As such, annuities can provide significantly better inheritance characteristics than non-annuity money without requiring a trust to accomplish those estate planning goals.

However, qualified accounts (IRAs, etc.) also are tax-deferred accounts that if set up with designated beneficiaries automatically bypass probate, requiring no trust to accomplish those two advantages. Accordingly, one might argue that putting qualified money in an annuity sacrifices those advantages and therefore is not a great idea. If tax-deferral and probate avoidance were the only justifications for owning the annuity, that would be correct. But, as it turns out, there are other compelling reasons to consider some annuity products as holding vehicles for IRA money.

Some More Basics (And a Little Math)

Everyone fundamentally wants the same three things from every financial account: growth, safety and liquidity.

If there were a financial product that offered high growth with complete avoidance of down-side risk and no limit on cash availability, that would be as close to a perfect product as one could imagine. It doesn't exist. Growth, safety, liquidity: one must be traded off to get the other two. This is not to suggest you must completely sacrifice one to get the other two but it does mean some compromise and choices are necessary.

Think about this like a balance. Use "G" for growth, "S" for safety and "L" for liquidity.

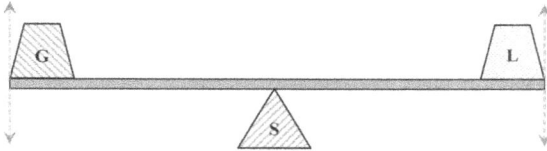

Select the variable most important. Let's assume you decide that's safety (S). Place S (safety) in the triangle (fulcrum = the balance point). Then place the other two variables (G for growth and L for liquidity) in the two side boxes, one each. When one side goes up the other goes down meaning, in this case, the more growth you want (goes up), the less liquidity you can have (goes down) or vice versa. By swapping the fulcrum variable, you can generate three sets of balance pairings, each with a fundamentally different base objective.

Good financial planning starts with what you can control. You cannot control what markets are going to do and the common practice of chasing returns is precisely that. You can control the pairing choices and then shop for products which conform to that combination.

Fundamentally, the financial services world consists of three industries: banking, securities and insurance. Each industry essentially correlates to one of the three pairings:

Banks pair liquidity with safety, the trade-off being growth.

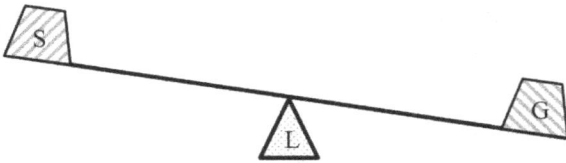

Securities typically pair growth (potential) with liquidity, trading off complete safety.

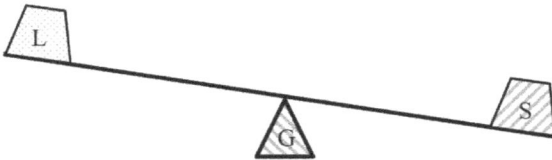

Insurance (fixed not variable annuities) pairs safety with growth, trading off unrestricted liquidity.

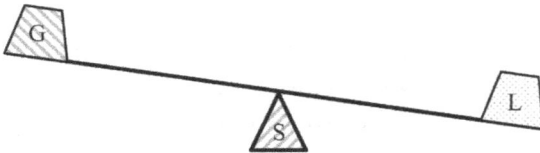

When it comes to qualified money, the significant advantage of tax-deferral ends at the required beginning age because from that point onward, money *must* be withdrawn every year (RMDs) and in most cases, it gets progressively larger (by percent) every single year. For example, the (new) standard table of RMDs mandates withdrawal of approximately 3.66% at age 72, approximately 3.92% at 75, approximately 4.93% at 80, etc. If anyone is fortunate enough to live to 120, the RMD schedule levels off at approximately 50%. I say "approximately" because the RMD table is based on a table of divisors, not percentage numbers, and the listed examples are the calculated percentages rounded to two decimal places. The actual calculations are easy with the table in hand, but you get the idea. The problem comes in *how and when* RMDs are calculated and *when* they're (usually) taken.

Every year, once a person reaches the required beginning age (70½ or 72) an RMD is determined based on the account value of December 31 of **last year** and applicable divisor based on a person's age on December 31 of **this year**. The RMD may be taken at any time during the year but most commonly it is taken toward year's end. However, the required amount, to the penny, is known and set as of December 31 of last year and regardless of what transpires in the markets, does not change.

Mathematically, account losses have a greater impact on the result than account gains of the same magnitude. The bigger the loss, the disproportionally bigger a gain is needed to "break even." For example, a 20% loss requires a 25% gain to offset it, a 35% loss requires a nearly 54% gain to offset and a loss of 50% requires a 100% gain to offset.

RMDs do not recalculate just because markets fall. For example, assume $100,000 IRA, 5% RMD (meaning $5000) and 30% market loss from January 2 to December 1 of the same year. Your $100,000 is now worth $70,000 but the RMD remains $5000. The sum of a 30% market drop plus 5% RMD reduces your account to $65,000 or 35% loss, now requiring 54% return before next year's RMD or the loss will be permanently etched in the account. If the IRA account also includes asset management fees, then those further compound the loss.

Ensuring an IRA Survives the Schedule of RMDs. Three Rules:

For our purposes here "surviving RMDs" will be taken to mean preservation of principal after the RMDs are withdrawn. In other words, if your IRA is worth $100,000 on your required beginning age, and it is still worth $100,000 on the date of your passing, the IRA "survived" the RMD schedule. Some people don't care if this is the case. Perhaps they have no heirs, have heirs they don't wish to provide inheritance for, or heirs who financially have no need for inheritance. For them, ensuring survival of the IRA may be of minimal importance. However, for the rest:

Rule #1 - An IRA in Required Minimum Distributions cannot be exposed to negative market risk.

For the reasons just demonstrated, if we accept the math and agree that Rule #1 has merit, then obviously equity (stock) market investments do not satisfy this rule. There is a reason that every security (investment) prospectus or other literature includes the disclaimer that the account "may lose value." This is not some idle "CYA" verbiage invented by lawyers. It's from FINRA and the SEC and exists because there really is no such thing as a security that is immune to stock market loss. Since the "invention" of stock exchanges (e.g., Frankfurt Stock Exchange in 1585), stock values at different times will rise, will fall and remain flat. They always have and they always will. People who deny this, or concoct some convoluted justification why they're immune or that it doesn't apply to them are playing a fool's game.

Therefore, let's accept the validity of Rule # 1. If so, where can someone put IRA money that is not exposed to market risk? Simply, it must be held in a principal-protected account. Most popularly, that means an insured fixed interest account such as a bank. Returning to the trifecta of variables (growth, safety, liquidity), the standard pairing offered by banks is safety and liquidity (at the expense of growth). If this isn't already obvious, try calling your bank and asking for a money market account paying 12% and see what happens.

Assuming a retiree who starts RMDs at 72 (current RMD table) and lives 20 years (to age 92) the schedule of RMDs will require an average annual return (without loss exposure) of slightly less than 5.7% to preserve principal. In the history of banking instruments such a thing has never occurred. Sure, there were a few exceptional years in the early 1980's with bank interest rates that great, but those periods were short-lived and on average (e.g., over a 20-year span), never happened. So...

Rule #2 – An IRA in Required Minimum Distributions must have enough growth to offset the RMDs.

The graph (below) illustrates the changes in a hypothetical account, starting with $100,000 after RMDs are deducted from ages 72 to 92.

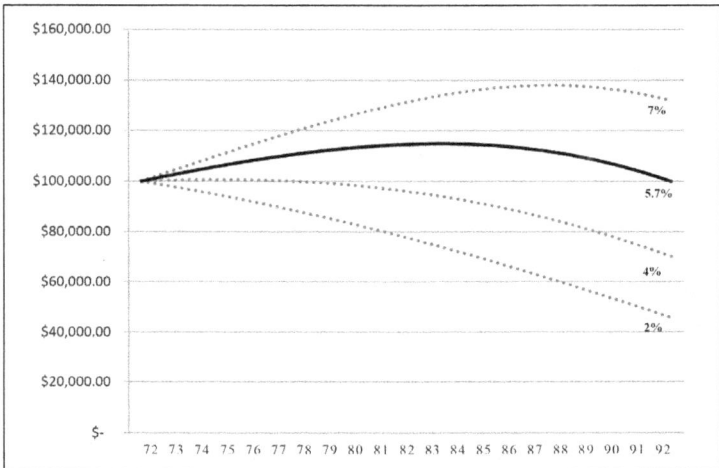

Notice that anything less than about 5.7% causes the account to lose value over time. In other words, for an IRA to survive the schedule of RMDs, it must average 5.7% annual return or more. That eliminates bank accounts, bonds and most other "safe" accounts.

Apart from the currently low interest rates, bonds aren't recommended because if (when) the RMD load exceeds bond coupons (which is certain to occur), the required withdrawal will necessitate liquidating some of the bond principal. If between the time of bond purchase and the time of liquidation, interest rates have risen, then the sale of bond shares will occur at a "discount" meaning a loss – in opposition to Rule #1.

What about annuities?
For an IRA to survive the schedule of RMDs, you must seek the combination of growth plus safety. That is a pairing that belongs to the insurance industry, meaning annuities – but be careful. Unfortunately, most annuities do **not** satisfy both Rules #1 and #2:

Variable Annuities have market risk and significant fees both of which compound account losses during times of market decline. Sure, some variable annuities have guaranteed minimum returns ("roll-ups" or guaranteed minimum withdrawal benefit riders) but functionally, they don't work as well as are popularly believed. It's because those features typically apply only to the generation of fixed lifetime income schedules (annuitization); not annual cash withdrawals which includes RMDs and in many (most?) cases, the roll-up guarantee terminates with any cash withdrawal (including an RMD). So variable annuities are out.

Fixed Interest Annuities offer guaranteed safe growth but at rates little better than bank accounts. Even back in the "good old days," when fixed interest annuities offered a lot higher guaranteed interest than presently, those multiyear guarantees were term-limited. Once the annuity reached its maturity date, the guaranteed rate typically reduced to a (low) stated minimum. So fixed interest annuities are out.

Fixed Indexed Annuities (FIAs) are a subset of fixed (not variable) annuities. The term indexed refers to the fact that these products rely on an external market index to determine growth. Functionally, you (the annuity owner) are NOT invested in the index (market) so you are never exposed to a market loss. You are credited with interest based on market index gains but never market losses. Any risk associated with negative markets is borne exclusively by the insurance company – not you. In fact, this is what the term "fixed" means so FIAs seem to comply with Rule #1.

Unfortunately, a great many FIAs impose secondary limitations on the growth potential. This is how they justify upside opportunity without downside risk. Most commonly these limitations come in the form of growth caps which are stated maximum amounts of growth that can be credited in any measurement period. For example, assume a FIA that links annual growth to the S&P 500 Index imposes an annual point-to-point cap of 4%. The annuity will compare the index value on the first and last days of a policy year and if the index has posted a net gain, apply that gain to the contract in the form of interest (called an index credit). If, for example, the S&P 500 posted a total gain of 3.5%, and your participation is 100% (meaning you get exactly what the growth was), your account will increase by 3.5%. If the S&P 500 experienced a loss, it does not count and you simply retain the same account value as before. But, is the S&P 500 posted a sizeable gain, say 15% or 20% and your growth cap is 4%, that's all you get: 4% and the rest doesn't count. It's not that the insurance company keeps the difference (that's not at all how it works). The added growth simply does not exist and nobody gets it. Years ago, growth caps were quite high (e.g., 15%) and those products would have fulfilled Rule #2. But today (2020), growth caps are nowhere close to those high values of yesterday and not likely to return. Worse is that when caps are imposed, the insurance company usually reserves the right to adjust the caps every year. Even if you started with a sufficiently high cap, there's no guarantee they'll remain that high. Therefore capped FIAs do not work.

Uncapped Fixed Index Annuities

Not all FIAs cap growth. At least at the time of writing, there are some which offer uncapped participation in market indexes with no downside risk. A few even do so with NO fees, NO buy-in costs, NO asset-management charges. No subtractions of any kind. Nothing.

Because different companies offer different products which can vary by state, a detailed description of those companies and products will not be provided here. To learn what may be available, please consult a licensed insurance representative, ideally one who is fully independent. However, I can say that (presently) the best of these products are not offered through "big name" brokerage firms, banks or even by captive insurance representatives. The carriers that offer the best of the best in the FIA space have the ability – if not luxury – to be highly selective about who gets to offer those products. Call it what you will, but when a company has a superior product or service, it can afford to be selective about who gets access. The good news, however, is that those limitations are imposed on agents and representatives, not on the general public seeking to purchase them.

On average, based on the past 10 to 20 years (depending no company and product), uncapped fixed index annuities have averaged roughly between 6% and 9% return per year. And while past performance can never be used as a promise of the future, at least historically, uncapped FIAs satisfy both Rule #1 and Rule #2 – and nothing else truly does.

Rule #3 – Reduce the Required Minimum Distribution.

This is a "rule" which, at first mention, is scoffed by most tax professionals as "impossible." After all, the table of RMDs is fixed and, barring an act of Congress, unchanging. Yet, as it turns out, a limited number of FIA products actually do reduce the net RMD load and accomplish this by virtue of a byproduct of their construction. The "trick" occurs when the annuity measures and credits growth to the account on a daily basis but locks in (secures) that growth after a multiple of years (e.g., two or three). It's called daily tracking with multi-year reset. Here's how it works: You make a deposit of, let's say $100,000. That's your principal and it's always protected. It's a floor below which your account can never fall (unless you physically withdraw money). Daily growth based on external measures of one or more market indices can increase or decrease your daily account value, but you can never fall below the floor. In that regard, it's just like being invested directly in the market except that the FIA's floor protects your principal. Then, every two years, three years (or whatever), the floor resets. If the total net indexed account value has gained, then your floor resets up to that new level. If the index has lost value, the previous floor preserves your account and the loss is not applied. Once the new floor is set, the measurement process repeats.

Because the annuity is defined as a principal-protected account and has no actual investment in the market index being measured, the IRS (by its own rules) can only charge an RMD against the principal-protected value (the floor), not the unrealized daily tracking value. Accordingly, in non-reset years the growth is effectively held in escrow in the daily tracked account. It is not included in the RMD calculation. That growth gets to grow and compound deferred from RMDs until the floor resets. In the meantime, the RMD is subtracted from the floor account so the next year's RMD is based on less because the previous RMD withdrawal reduced the floor and the growth didn't count toward that RMD calculation. Over time, the difference compounds and serves to *actually reduce the net average size of RMDs* and results in an increase in the total account value for no reason other than the RMDs averaged less.

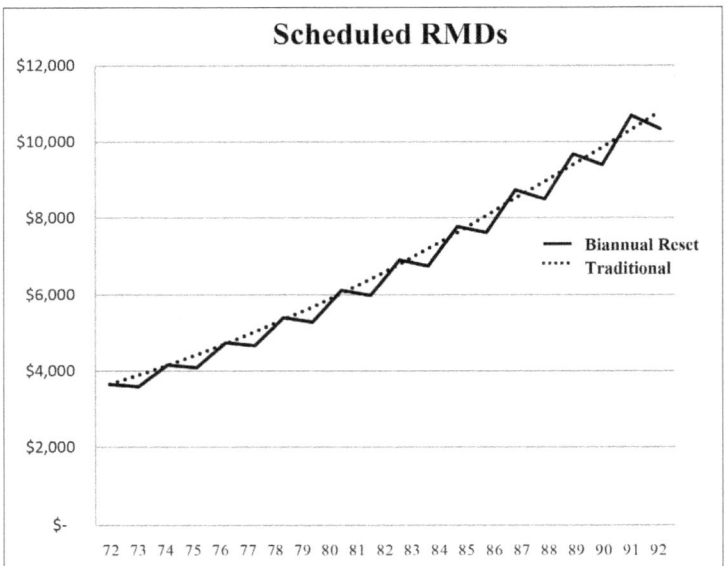

The traditional (dashed) line represents the increasing size of RMDs from age 72 to age 92. The solid (saw-toothed) represents a hypothetical uncapped FIA with biannual reset. Both models assume a level return of 6.0% per year. In the "even" (non-reset) years, the FIA forces a smaller RMD. The reason the reduced RMD and reset years are both "even"

is because RMDs always look back to last year's account value. The "space" between the solid and dashed lines represents money that was NOT withdrawn and therefore gets to compound for another year.

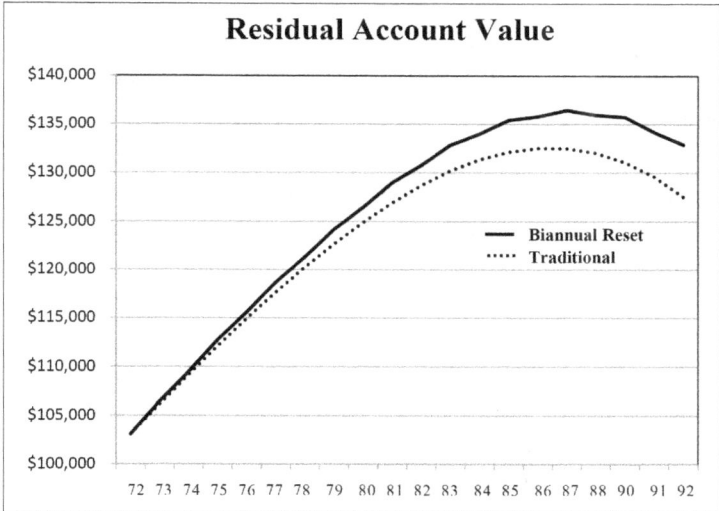

Residual Account Value

The result of this saw-toothing is that the FIA account grows and compounds at a greater rate than any other account type. Or put another way, it reduces the necessary minimum amount of growth for the IRA account to preserve its principal in the face of RMDs.

Only uncapped fixed index annuities with daily tracking and multi-year reset satisfy Rules #1, #2 and #3.

Tax and Other Considerations

It's been said that money is either for you or not for you. There's no "gray area" in that one. You don't get to keep the money you spend and you don't get to take what you don't spend with you when you go.

Money for You

Let's return to our 3 ideal variables: growth, safety, liquidity. Many people have portfolios of IRA money, non-IRA money and even Roth IRA money. Because of taxes, most people will be least likely to take cash out of the IRA (taxed as ordinary income) as opposed to take money from the Roth (not taxed at all) or from the non-IRA account (gains taxed at the favorable Long Term rate). Therefore, IRA money is (and should be) considered the least liquid (specifically for discretionary purposes) of the three. Given three accounts of identical size: IRA, non-IRA and Roth IRA, the sequence of greatest to least liquidity is Roth IRA first, non-IRA second and IRA last. Conversely, for income generation, the IRA should be the first, the Roth IRA second and the non-IRA last. If this seems self-contradictory, consider the following: Only the IRA has a mandatory liquidation schedule that is fully taxable. You have no choice. Therefore, if you rely on that RMD as an income source, you get to preserve and grow, as much as possible, the less tax-burdened accounts for discretionary use (meaning things that you decide to do from time-to-time after paying your monthly bills). As we'll see in another chapter, strategic use of RMDs and Social Security and other non-taxable income sources can minimize – or even eliminate owing income tax on anything – including the RMDs.

If you need more income than what comes from Social Security, Pension and RMDs, then ideally, use your Roth IRA first. Remember, not only is Roth income not taxed, it does not count "against" the calculation of how much of your Social Security is taxed. Even tax-free income from qualified dividends or municipal bonds counts against Social Security taxability.

Finally, if you still need more, especially to cover occasional larger ticket needs (or you don't have a Roth IRA), then withdraw from the non-IRA account. Your principal won't be taxed and your gains will (likely) be taxed at the more favorable long term capital gains rate. If your AGI is below certain thresholds (e.g., $80,000 for a couple in 2020), the long term capital gains tax rate is 0%. How much tax you ultimately owe will be determined by a number of factors including total taxable income and deductions. This is where seeking advice from a tax-planning professional (CPA, tax attorney, etc.) is invaluable.

So back to growth, safety and liquidity: Uncapped fixed index annuities combine growth (potential) and safety better than any other product category. So what about liquidity? Annuities, particularly fixed index annuities are time deposits. You put the money in and are expected to leave it alone for an extended period of time – how long depends on the company and product but it's not a matter of one or two years. However, that's not to say that the money is "locked up" and unavailable. Rather, annuities – the good ones at least – offer penalty-free access to the money, commonly after one year, sometimes with no time restrictions at all. RMDs are always paid out with no penalty imposed and if more is desired, more can (usually) be taken penalty-free – up to the full limit of penalty-free availability. In addition, many FIA contracts permit penalty-free surrender for certain major medical events and always as a death benefit.

In light of all this, it becomes clearer that the potential "downside" of limited liquidity in uncapped FIAs is not so significant (who would liquidate a large IRA in lump sum if they had non-IRA (or Roth IRA) funds to withdraw from)?

Money NOT for You

When an IRA is inherited, it must be liquidated starting the year after death and it is always reported as taxable ordinary income. In other words, IRA money is 100% taxable to you and to your heirs. This is true whether the money is in an annuity or not. The annuity offers no direct tax advantages nor added tax liabilities when the money is IRA.

When a Roth IRA is inherited, it too must be liquidated starting the year after death according to the same liquidation schedules as an inherited IRA. However, it is not taxed upon receipt.

When a non-IRA is inherited, it (currently) receives a step-up in basis meaning the basis (or "acquisition value") becomes equal to the value on the date of death (or possibly an alternative date up to six months after). In other words, inherited non-IRA money may be liquidated with no income tax consequences but does not have to be. Other than life insurance, there is no better way to inherit money than from a non-IRA account.

However, when non-IRA money is in an annuity, these advantages go away. Because annuities grow money tax-deferred, whenever the money is received, the gains are taxed as ordinary income. In addition, annuities must be liquidated upon inheritance by anyone other than a spouse. Therefore, many of the tax advantages of non-IRA money are lost when non-IRA funds are in an annuity. This is not the case with IRA or Roth IRA money.

Think about IRA, Non-IRA and Roth IRA as three distinct buckets of money. The way each is taxed to you, to your heirs and the presence or absence of mandatory withdrawals (RMDs) makes them very different.

	IRA	Non-IRA		Roth IRA
YOU	100% taxed as ordinary income **RMD** mandated	**Annuity:** Gains taxed as ordinary income	**Non-Annuity:** Gains taxed LTCG (lower rate)	0 tax No RMD
HEIRS	100% taxed as ordinary income **RMD** mandated	**Annuity:** Gains taxed as ordinary income **RMD** mandated	**Non-Annuity:** 0 tax (step-up) No RMD	0 tax **RMD** mandated

From a practical standpoint, other than their RMDs, IRAs are less liquid than either non-IRA or Roth IRA money. That plus the growth and safety concerns, it is easy to see why IRAs best fit the growth plus safety pairing meaning uncapped FIAs.

From a tax standpoint, Roth IRA money is more desirable than non-IRA money, meaning that it should have the most liquidity to you. However, because there is a mandatory distribution upon inheritance from Roth IRA but not from non-IRA which is also not taxed at inheritance, the non-IRA money is a bit more advantageous for inheritance and the Roth IRA money is a bit better for you. In both these cases, non-annuity accounts may be more attractive, particularly with the non-IRA money that is taxed more heavily to you and to your heirs.

There are times when it makes sense to have non-IRA money in annuities – and times when IRA money should NOT. However, a balanced investment portfolio that seeks to include a reasonable mix of both annuities and non-annuities may be benefitted by this general arrangement.

Chapter 10

INHERITING IRAS

Prior to passage of the SECURE Act, an inherited IRA was permitted to be "stretched" meaning liquidated according to the life expectancy of the beneficiary. Effective January 1, 2020, with limited exceptions, all inherited IRAs (to other than a spouse) must be fully liquidated within 10 years.

Presently, the law provides the following exceptions to the ten-year liquidation rule:

1. A Spouse may combine an inherited IRA with his or her own and treat the required distribution schedule accordingly.

2. A minor child may defer taking distributions until 18, after which the 10-year rule applies.

3. A beneficiary who is disabled, chronically ill or not more than 10 years younger than the IRA owner. In these cases, the IRA may be distributed over the beneficiary's life expectancy.

4. Qualified annuity contract wherein the annuity schedule is established as a binding annuity contract in effect not later than December 31, 2019.

A number of planning implications may be derived from this law change.

1. **Small IRA:** If a person has a relatively small IRA (e.g., under $100,000) and/or a lot of beneficiaries, the 10-year rule will not likely be burdensome. For example, one beneficiary per $100,000 of inherited IRA means that the annual inheritance for each beneficiary will be $10,000 (plus whatever growth occurred). That's not likely going to create an added income tax burden.

2. **Minor Child:** If a minor child inherits an IRA, he/she will be permitted to defer distributions until age 18. However, most 18 year olds are just finishing high school and entering college. During their education years, few students are earning enough income to be taxed. With the standard deduction (as of 2020) at $12,400 per person, any inherited IRA distributions below that threshold (including any income) are not taxed at all and above that to $22,275 of total income ($9,875 tier + $12,400 deduction) is taxed at the 10% bracket. In addition, if the parent is providing at least half of the child's financial support, the parents may take the dependent deduction. All this adds up to a simple conclusion that there may be value in naming grandchildren as IRA beneficiaries. Not only does the inherited IRA have a chance of being received partially, or entirely untaxed, the parents get to enjoy a deduction from their income taxes (although not related to the inherited IRA).

3. **Strategic conversion** by the IRA owner of the IRA to Roth (Roth conversion) or to non-qualified accounts prior to inheritance. Either version results in a conversion of a taxable inheritance to a non-taxable inheritance. The key is to structure the conversion to not cross the threshold

into higher tax brackets. For example, suppose Sam and Beth, both 60, have IRAs worth $750,000. Their combined income is $100,000. They are currently at the 22% top marginal tax bracket (above $19,750 and below $171,050 as married, filing joint for 2020). By converting $75,000 per year to either Roth IRA or non-IRA, they increase their taxable income to $175,000. But because they have a $24,800 standard deduction, they don't cross into the 24% bracket until their income exceeds $195,850. Over the next 10 years, they can successfully convert the entirety of their IRAs to non-taxable accounts without adding to the tax rate. In addition, by the time they are 70 and starting Social Security, they will have no impending danger that RMDs (at 72 and beyond) will impact the taxability of their Social Security benefits.

Fundamentally there are two variations of strategic conversion:

Version 1. Roth Conversion. Current tax code permits an IRA to be converted into a Roth IRA without regard to a person's income or net worth. Tax on the liquidated money is due but with good planning, many people can strategically convert an IRA to a Roth without significantly increasing their income tax load. However, the decision to convert, and the amounts to be converted, are questions to ask a financial planning professional or a CPA. There are times when making a Roth conversion is a good idea, and times when it is not. For example, if a person completes the Roth conversion before electing Social Security benefits, then the annual conversions do not add to the taxability of the Social Security payments. Conversely, if the conversion is done after the RBA, the conversion amounts and the required minimum distributions are additive (conversion amounts do not count as RMDs) and the tax load increases, on both the withdrawals and on Social Security benefits. There are a myriad of additional considerations.

However, one of the biggest values of the Roth conversion is if the account owner plans to use the money for future big ticket items (e.g., medical expenses or long term care). Withdrawing large sums of money from any other type of account (traditional IRA or non-IRA, etc.) can generate a taxable consequence. In years past, there was the possibility of offsetting some of the potential tax consequences with a medical expense deduction but under current tax law, that is functionally off the table. Withdrawing large sums from a Roth IRA does not result in a taxable event and does not even count toward the taxability of Social Security.

Version 2. Non-IRA Conversion. The value of converting to a non-IRA account (including not Roth) is greater when inheritance is the primary objective. Inherited non-IRA (and non-annuity) funds receive a step-up in basis, meaning their acquisition value is the same as the value on the date of death. Thus, if an heir sells the inherited asset, there is no income tax exposure. As such, this makes it similar to an inherited Roth except the Roth has a 10-year liquidation mandate and the non-IRA does not. Therefore, inheriting a non-IRA account offers a bit more flexibility and choice to the beneficiary than inheriting a Roth.

4. **Gift to Charity:** Someone with an IRA that they simply don't want or need can make an outright gift to a designated charitable entity (501(c)(3) Organization) and avoid the tax. The charity doesn't pay tax either. However, you do

not get a tax deduction for the gift. It's simply a gift without strings attached and you get the satisfaction of knowing your money is helping an organization you care about.

5. **Life Insurance:** For inheritance purposes, few things are more efficient than life insurance. The benefit is paid rapidly and income tax free. It bypasses probate and has the highest risk-free return of any account. And it can be structured (through a life insurance trust) to withhold or control distribution according to a specific set of conditions or instructions of the owner's choosing. If the estate is large (and exposed to possible estate or inheritance taxes), a life insurance trust is perhaps the easiest (best) way to bypass that tax exposure. In addition to the previously noted benefits, one important advantage of life insurance conversion is the leverage. A healthy person, depending on age, can build a very substantial inheritance for relatively few dollars. Even more, the policy can be obtained by spending only the IRA growth, thereby preserving principal in the IRA while leveraging for the insurance. All the previous strategies merely swap an account from the "left pocket" to the "right pocket."

In addition, life insurance can be funded through a specified schedule of premiums for a limited period of time, after which no further payments are required. However, the death benefit is permanent (we're NOT talking about term insurance here) and once paid for, leaves the IRA available to be manipulated by any of the previously mentioned strategies. In other words, starting with the life insurance program does not mean giving up another strategy either presently or later.

Choosing the right type of life insurance. The type of life insurance policy you select is also significant. The key is to get a permanent policy; not term which may be cheap but will very likely lapse (end) before you do. If you're single, the most attractive type of policy is probably a universal life policy. Similar to whole life in that it is a cash-accumulating permanent policy, universal life policies tend to be less expensive for the same benefit amount, particularly when larger than $100,000 of death benefit.

For married couples, one of the more advisable approaches is to fund a SUL (Survivor Universal Life) policy. A SUL insures two people as though one and pays the benefit after the second passes (also known as a "Second-to-Die" policy). From an estate planning perspective, there are several advantages:

1. Insuring two people is less expensive than one. This means the death benefit amount is greater for the same premium dollar than would be the case for either of the couple individually.

   For example, a healthy male, age 60 wants to convert his $300,000 IRA into tax-free inheritance. He determines that he can withdraw 10% ($30,000) per year, pay 20% tax and allocate the balance to premiums ($2,000 per month) for ten years, then make no more payments. He will get an insurance policy worth about $700,000 that will be inherited income tax free. However, if that man is married and, for example, his wife is also 60 and healthy, that same $2,000 per month for just 10 years can buy a SUL policy with a death benefit of $1,000,000 or more.

2. The benefit is paid income tax-free to heirs at the precise time they need to cover any final expenses and avoids probate.

3. The policy may be funded in such a way that the premium payments count as or toward satisfying the RMDs.

The policy and premium schedule may be structured to preserve the principal value of IRA, retaining those funds in the name of the owner for potential future need, and even stretched if that provision remains permitted.

4. **Trust Planning:** IRAs cannot be placed in a trust. Doing so will result in an immediate taxable event on the entire account. However, good trust planning can be effected using IRA money as a resource. Two examples are offered as illustrative. Others exist. Any trust planning should ultimately be designed by an estate planning attorney

Special Needs Trust. If you have an intended beneficiary who has special needs, particularly if they are receiving Medicaid benefits and there is a concern that inheriting a large sum of money might disrupt that benefit, a special needs trust can offer a viable way to provide for them without disrupting their government assistance benefits. Once the trust is established (drafted), it must be funded. Using IRA money to fund a Special Needs Trust will result in a taxable event to you, but then, the moneys are tax-advantaged when payable to the trust beneficiary. In particular, the use of life insurance as the funding vehicle within the trust is highly advantageous. This is because of the leveraging of premium to death benefit amount and it becomes an effective means of using an IRA that is unneeded for personal income

Spendthrift Trust. Even if your heir(s) are not special needs but are simply terrible with money, placing funds inside a trust that controls when and how much they receive can be an important aspect of financial planning. Because of RMDs, neither an IRA nor a Roth IRA can easily function in this capacity, but a trust funded with an insurance policy can and as already noted, spending an IRA down as the source of premiums is an effective way of funding the trust while reducing tax exposure on an inherited IRA, especially if the beneficiary is a poor money manager.

IRAs were never designed to be inheritance accounts. Rather their purpose was to be a source of retirement income. It is therefore not surprising that Congress took steps to diminish the inheritance value of them – particularly in light of our nation's large, ballooning deficit. Still, there are many retirees who simply do not need the RMD income and want to minimize tax exposure. Regardless of what new laws Congress passes, there are always ways to plan to maximize individual benefits. The key is to do strategic planning.

Chapter 11

IRAS AND MEDICAID QUALIFICATION

N obody likes to think about getting sick but the need for long term care is a fact of life for a significant portion of the country's elderly. According to a U.S. Department of Health and Human Services report (2016), about 52% of Americans turning 65 will need some form of long term care and one in seven (14%) will need that care for at least five years. Long term care is not medical care. Rather it is custodial care for people who cannot care for themselves for the most basic of needs without substantial assistance: eating, dressing, bathing, personal hygiene, moving around and going to the bathroom. In simple terms, it's a return to those earliest days of life when you were too young to care for yourself with one important distinction: you grew up. There are three major myths about long term care need:

1. **Myth 1:** *"My family will take care of me."* Unless your family members are willing to give up their personal lives 24/7, have professional training and specialized equipment, this is a naive if not dangerous notion (not

to mention horrifically unfair). Don't believe me? Try lying down on the floor in your living room and ask your intended care-giving family member to pick you up carry you to the bedroom and place you gently on the bed. Now expect them to do that morning, noon and night, Monday through Sunday for months or even years with no let up.

2. **Myth 2:** *"I'll just kill myself."* Nonsense. You had a stroke (or similar). You can't get out of bed and move around by yourself. You can't fix your food or take your medication without assistance. How exactly are you going to commit suicide? Attempting – and failing – will only make the problem worse. Plus, if you try to include anybody else in any capacity in that plan, whether successful or not, it will subject them to a relatively serious felony prosecution.

3. **Myth 3:** *"Medicare will pay."* Sorry, but not true. At BEST, Medicare will pay for the first 20 days of facility-based long term care need – IF you entered the Nursing Home on doctor's orders after a qualified hospital stay within 30 days of your hospital release. After that, Medicare will pay the next 80 days after you pay a daily copay of $176.00 (2020 rate). After that, you're entirely on your own.

There are three ways to pay for a Long Term Care need:

a. **You pay.** People with substantial assets can do this but the average cost of a Long Term Care need which is highly dependent on where you live, is in the range of $75,000 to $150,000 per year for typically about two to three years.

b. **Insurance pays**. Long Term Care insurance, while the most reliable way to cover the need can be quite expensive (or unavailable), especially for people who wait until things start to go wrong. However, there are a number of different Long Term Care strategies available through different insurance products (including certain life insurance or annuity products) that can be used to reduce the out-of-pocket cost for the protection.

c. **State Pays**. In other words, you seek state financial assistance from Medicaid.

Medicaid qualification for long term care is a highly complex and grossly misunderstood process. The rules differ state-by-state and are in a continual state of flux. For those reasons, this book will not seek to inform beyond rudimentary basics and instead urge that anyone with current or pending long term care, who cannot be fully covered by insurance or personal wealth, should consult an Elder Law Attorney.

First, more myth-busting: There are two general myths about Medicaid qualification.

Myth 1: Medicaid takes everything you have. Actually, Medicaid takes nothing from you. What happens is that Medicaid has money to give and, in effect, they either say "yes" (they will give some) or "no" (they won't). If they say "no" you get no money from Medicaid and you're on your own to pay the cost of care which can be incredibly expensive. The facilities have a simple rule: *"No pay, no stay."* But they will allow you to liquidate assets to pay for the care and this is called "spend-down." Spend down is where families lose everything, not because Medicaid took it, but because it was sold to pay for the care. Medicaid said "no" and didn't offer to pay so you did.

Myth 2: You must be broke to qualify for Medicaid (to get Medicaid to say "yes"). This is a gross over simplification. Technically, Medicaid is supposed to help people who financially cannot help themselves, but the blanket notion that you must be broke is incorrect. There are actually several different versions of financial assistance under Medicaid, depending on a number of variables. Apart from different levels of Medicaid qualification, Medicaid also recognizes a difference between the spouse who needs care ("institutionalized spouse") and the spouse who does not ("community" or "at home spouse"). Medicaid qualification then applies two types of financial tests which always involve the institutionalized spouse and sometimes the community spouse.

Financial Test 1: Asset Limits Test - Medicaid recognizes assets as either "countable" or "non-countable." Countable assets are those which are included in determining the maximum allowable assets to qualify for financial assistance. In some cases, that is not more than $2,000. In other cases, more and allowances differ for institutionalized vs. community spouses. "Non-countable" assets do not count regardless of how big. For example, a primary residence is non-countable if under a specified value ($500,000 in most states; $750,000 in some). In other words, it doesn't matter how much the house is worth, as long as it's not worth more than the maximum allowed amount. Being worth too much, if even by $1, makes an otherwise non-countable asset, countable. And Medicaid gets to determine how the property is appraised: commonly but not necessarily by tax value.

A big part of Medicaid qualification planning centers around maximizing non-countable assets, minimizing Countable Assets and, where possible, converting countable into non-countable assets sufficient to pass the asset limits test. There are legal ways to do this but unfortunately, many of the ideas that people have are not permissible. The most common strategy that does not work is giving assets away. That even includes things like selling the house for $1. Any transfer of an asset for less than fair market value is considered a gift. For example, you have a house worth $250,000 and you "sell" it to your son for $1. You just made a gift of $249,999.

Warning: Improperly retitling (gifting) countable assets to *anyone*, other than permitted with narrow allowances, can result in a moratorium on approval. Part of the application and approval process is a five year look-back to see if you made disqualifying gifts. If so, that moratorium is applied forward from the date of Medicaid application.

Financial Test 2: Income Limits Test - Under this test, Medicaid looks at the income for both institutional and community spouses. In some cases, having "too much" income can result in non-approval of the application ("no"). In other cases, it does not disqualify the application, but rather reduces how much Medicaid actually pays. For example, Medicaid may say *"Yes, we'll give you money, but only after you pay the first $_____."* In some types of Medicaid qualification, Medicaid may restrict how much income the community spouse may have; in others, not.

In short, Medicaid qualification for long term care is a very complex and a highly convoluted process. If you do it wrong and get denied, no problem, you simply must go to the back of the line and refile (maybe). Of course, that can take months (or years) and in the meantime, guess who pays for the care? (Beginning to see why Medicaid qualification requires professional counsel?)

Medicaid Qualification and Qualified Plans

This book is about IRAs so let's focus on this important component because they require special consideration.

One popular strategy for converting countable to non-countable assets is transfer ownership from the institutionalized to community spouse. With most property and non-qualified accounts, this is relatively easy, but not IRAs. A qualified account cannot have joint ownership and any transfer of a qualified account (other than Roth) to anyone other than the original owner, will generate a taxable event, including possibly a tax penalty. This makes handling qualified money (IRAs, etc.) a very delicate matter when it comes to Medicaid qualification.

There are a number of false and misleading articles about this out there. Some suggest that an IRA in standard required minimum distributions makes it non-countable asset. It doesn't. Medicaid rules permit an account being liquidated to remain non-countable only if the account meets certain narrow requirements. These qualifications are most reliably met by the use of a "Medicaid qualified annuity" (sometimes "Medicaid compliant annuity"). But any old annuity will not work. To be effective, the annuity must:

1. Completely convert the IRA account to an income that is not revocable and not transferable. If there is any way that at a future date, the annuity income can be modified or terminated, the account remains countable.

2. Be "actuarially sound" meaning it is an income for a finite number of years based on a reasonable life expectancy (Medicaid has its own life expectancy tables). It is based on the life of the income recipient (not the institutional spouse) and cannot be payable to the Medicaid applicant (institutional spouse). Essentially, the income must be payable to the community spouse.

3. Name the state's Medicaid office as a contingent beneficiary (meaning the second-in-line beneficiary after the income beneficiary recipient. In "plain English," Medicaid is saying *"We'll let you care for your spouse but we're not going to give you our money so you can give yours to your kids."*

As already stated, the rules differ state by state; some may be more forgiving and others less than described here. If you're now thinking *"I'll move to a better state to qualify,"* don't. Doing so may invalidate your ability to qualify altogether.

The point is that anyone who remotely may need to consider Medicaid qualification (even if you personally abhor the idea), really needs to be very careful about exactly where their IRA money is invested. Some assets (and asset classes) are more "friendly" than others when it comes to making adjustments to qualify for benefits. The sad truth is that painfully few financial advisors know enough about the nuances of Medicaid qualification to offer even the most rudimentary of advice.

To summarize, *never, ever* attempt Medicaid qualification on your own without professional assistance from a competent Elder Law Attorney.

Chapter 12

IRAS AND JUDGMENTS IN COURT

W e exist in a very litigious time. Anyone with sizeable assets lives with a large target on their backs. You need not have actually done anything wrong to become the subject of a lawsuit and win or lose, it's an expensive proposition. In particular, people with rental properties are at risk, but so are folks with raw, undeveloped land or even large investment accounts. The good news is that there are a number of relatively simple ways to protect yourself against litigation. The easiest is to have an umbrella policy. Obtained from your regular home insurer, a million dollars of coverage is available for a couple hundred dollars per year. However, just because you have one million dollars in coverage doesn't mean you can't get sued for two million, or if you have two million in coverage, that you can't get sued for four.

Estate planning and asset protection attorneys can offer additional protection through the use of business structures and trusts that are very effective, but these can cost money to establish and maintain. While these strategies may protect against litigation, they may not be so effective for bankruptcy, divorce settlement, court-ordered child support, etc.

However, most qualified plans are governed by ERISA which affords an automatic measure of protection. In most states, IRAs and similar are exempted from legal judgment, including bankruptcy, divorce, etc. However, the rules differ widely state-by-state. They also differ by type of qualified plan. For example, you may live in a state that provides complete exemption for your 401(k) plan, partial exemption for your traditional IRA and no exemption for your Roth IRA. If you live in a state where one or more of these plans are not exempted, and you have a judgment entered against you, those plans could be garnished for repayment and if you were relying on those plans for your retirement, that plan could be placed in jeopardy.

At least as of January 2014 the following summary from "The Tax Advisor" (https://www.thetaxadviser.com/content/dam/tta/issues/2014/jan/stateirachart.pdf) offers insight into the degree of variation among states. However, state laws can and do change and thus the following summary is intended to illustrate the disparity of rules among different states; not provide state-specific advice. Anyone seeking specific information should consult an attorney licensed to practice *in that state.*

Alaska: Amounts contributed to a qualified plan within 120 days before debtor files for bankruptcy are not exempt.

Arizona: Claims under a Qualified Domestic Relations Order are not exempt.

California: IRAs are only exempt when necessary to support the judgment debtor or support for spouse and dependents. Roth IRAs are not exempt.

Colorado: There is no exemption for late child support payments or for murder.

Delaware: Claims under a Qualified Domestic Relations Order are not exempt.

Florida: Claims under a Qualified Domestic Relations Order are not exempt nor, in some cases, are claims for a surviving spouse.

Georgia: IRAs are only exempt to the extent necessary for support of the debtor and dependents. Roth IRAs are not exempt.

Hawaii: Contributions made three or fewer years before civil action is initiated are not exempt.

Idaho: Claims due to negligent or other wrongful acts resulting in money damages are not exempt.

Kentucky: Contributions within 120 days of bankruptcy filing or court-ordered child support are not exempt.

Maine: IRAs are exempt to $15,000 or "reasonably necessary" for child support. Roth IRAs are not exempt.

Massachusetts: The exemption does not apply to court-orders for divorce, child support or monetary restitution for criminal activity or other exceptions.

Michigan: Deposits made within 120 days of bankruptcy filing are not exempt.

Minnesota: The exemption is limited to a present value of $69,000.

Mississippi: IRAs are exempt; Roth IRAs are not.

Montana: Contributions within one year of filing are not exempt. Roth IRAs are not exempt.

Nebraska: IRAs are partly exempt; Roth IRAs are not.

Nevada: The exemption is limited to a present value of $500,000.

New Mexico: The exemption applies to persons supporting themselves.

New York: Contributions made within 90 days of filing are not exempt.

North Dakota: An exemption applies to first $100,000 for an individual or $200,000 for a couple.

Ohio: SEP and SIMPLE plans are not exempt.

Pennsylvania: Contributions more than $15,000 made in the year before filing are not exempt.

Rhode Island: Divorce or child support claims are not exempt. Inherited IRAs are exempt.

Tennessee: Claims under a Qualified Domestic Relations Order are not exempt.

Utah: Contributions made within one year of filing are not exempt.

Vermont: Nondeductible contributions to an IRA, including earnings, are not exempt.

West Virginia: Roth IRAs are not exempt.

Wisconsin: Child support or family support orders are not exempt.

Wyoming: Partial exemptions may apply to both IRA and Roth accounts.

States not listed provide broad exemption to all qualified accounts.

Chapter 13

FUTURE CONSIDERATIONS

T he laws governing qualified accounts do change from time-to-time. In most cases, those changes are relatively minor. However, in some cases, they can be significant. For example, the Economic Growth and Tax Relief Reconciliation Act of 2001 reduced the RMD load. That new RMD table remains the one effect until the new proposed table (2019) takes effect.

In 2016, the Department of Labor announced substantial changes to how advisors handled accounts qualified under ERISA. The changes were not implemented through legislation but by DOL directive and were believed by many in the financial services world to be very damaging to both the advisors and clients. Before it could fully take effect, the DOL Fiduciary Rule was vacated by the courts. Nonetheless, it was a stark reminder how tenuous laws that govern qualified accounts can be.

In 2017, Congress passed one of the most substantial tax revision plans in a generation.

In 2019, the SECURE Act passed, which among other things, substantially changed when RMDs must begin and how inherited IRAs are handled.

There are but two certainties regarding tax laws. 1. They will always exist in some form and 2. they will eventually be modified. Beyond that, any attempt to predict future changes in law is a fool's game. Accordingly, the best strategy – the only strategy – is to proceed based on what is current and remain prepared in case there is a change. To paraphrase Yogi Berra: "*It ain't law 'til it's law*."

In general, people commit one of two fundamental mistakes in their planning.

1. The "*I don't know anything about this*" crowd avoids planning out of fear and confusion. Overwhelmed by the unknown, they do whatever someone tells them – often a friend or family member and then never think about it again. This approach is flawed on many fronts. First it assumes the friend or family member is not only a financial planning authority, but is also fully licensed with access to and has detailed knowledge of the complete breadth of possible solutions – including the latest innovations. Second, it presumes that everyone's needs and circumstances are identical (The cookie-cutter approach of "*What's good for me is good for you*."). Finally, it assumes that planning is a "one-and-done" proposition. But none of this is in a person's best interest. Fear and confusion about the unknown does not solve the problem of poor, or no advice. Mistakes cost and good intentions do not count.

2. On the other hand, there are the do-it-yourselfers. These self-described, self-promoting "private experts" somehow

know more than professionals in the field, occasionally including the world's foremost authorities – even Nobel Laureate Economists – yet they hold no professional licenses and have no formal training. When queried, these folks invariably profess that they self-advise because they believe they can out-perform professional managers and do so for a fraction of the costs. That might be valid if only it were true. Unfortunately, there's plenty of research to demonstrate it's not. In fact, based on extensive research, more often than not, active traders underperform more conservative long-term investors. There are a number of reasons for this:

a. Private (meaning do-it-yourself) investors do not have access to the type and level of research available to professional fund managers.

b. Private investors do not have access to the wide array of investment and financial products that require licensing to obtain.

c. Markets, particularly in contemporary times, move rapidly and in response to unpredictable events. For example, from October 29 to November 7, 2018, the Dow Jones Industrial Average (Dow) gained 1737.38 points. Then from November 7 through November 23, lost 1894.35 points. From November 23 through December 3 gained 1540.48 points and from December 3 through December 24 lost 4034.23 points. By January 17, had recovered to the same level as on October 29.

d. Day trading is an attempt to "beat the markets." Even if successful on paper, it "conveniently" ignores the transactional costs and if in non-qualified accounts, taxes associated with those trades.

e. Sequence of timing concerns. A lot of research (e.g., DALBAR Research Group) has shown that consistently, because active traders are reactive rather than proactive, their subsequent trades are invariably a little behind the curve. In other words, while the ideal is "buy low and sell high" by not being able to react as rapidly as markets move, they're invariably "buying high and selling low" and as a consequence, under-perform the markets.

f. Chasing returns. Everyone loves returns but focusing only on that variable ignores another of equal importance: probability. The notion of a risk-adjusted return accounts for both variables: average return as the objective (what everyone wants) and risk which measures the chance of actually achieving that objective. Consider the following: The greatest potential return is a lottery ticket (spend $5, gain $50 million) but the risk (chance of failure) is very high. In fact, it is statistically 100%. In 1964 and 1966, Stanford University professor of economics William F. Sharpe published two papers that sought to quantify the relationship of these two variables. He was awarded the Nobel Prize in Economic Sciences for his work (primarily the Capital Asset Pricing Model). Subsequently, there have been numerous additional variations of risk-adjusted return calculations. However, for practical purposes, I propose one to be called a "Risk-weighted Return." Very simply it is the ratio of the return divided by the risk (always converted to a positive number), times the return. For example, assume two investments with an average annual return of 8%. But one has a risk of 16% (the standard deviation) and the other has a risk of 6%.

Investment A would have a Risk-weighted Return of 4% because the risk is twice the return and the equation discounts the expected return proportionally. Conversely Investment B would have a risk-weighted return of 10.67% because having risk less than the return offers a premium return. Clearly a choice of 10.67% is better than 4% and by simply chasing raw returns (8% each) would leave the investor unclear as to which, A or B is actually better.

In summary, sound investing is – or should be – done with a long-term view and in full consideration of facts. With rare exception, accepting advice from anyone other than a trained, licensed professional (including oneself) is not likely to provide the best result. Once choices are made, they should be periodically reviewed. In most cases, that means annually or when significant changes in a financial picture occur.

When people make sound decisions based on long-term objectives, the short-term fluctuations are less relevant. This view of planning offers a more reliable platform for retirement and relieves stress. Qualified plans – if properly structured and managed, can (and do) provide a valuable supplement in retirement. If mismanaged, qualified accounts can be burdensome, especially in light of income taxes and inheritance.

Albert Einstein is quoted as having said "*Never memorize something that you can look up.*" A corollary of this might be to "*Seek knowledge from the most reliable sources.*" When it comes to financial matters, seek advice from those who are professionally trained and licensed. However, do a bit of homework on what that means. Getting a basic insurance or securities license is not difficult and conveys little if anything about that advisor's practical knowledge and expertise. An advisor who has invested the time and effort in obtaining professional certifications or higher-than basic licenses is in a position to offer more than one who has only the most basic and rudimentary of licensing.

Tips for Selecting a Professional Advisor

Make sure your advisor is:

- **A Fiduciary** is someone who is held to a higher standard and by law, must make recommendations based on what is in the client's best interest, not the representative's or the rep's employer. In 2019, the SEC created Regulation Best Interest (BI) which requires broker-dealers to only recommend financial products in the best interest of clients and to clearly identify any potential conflicts of interest. In other words, to adhere to a Fiduciary role. Regulation BI also mandated that only licensed Investment Advisors (e.g., Registered Investment Advisor) may call themselves "Advisors" because only they are legally bound as financial Fiduciaries.

- **Fully independent** meaning has no contractual or employment allegiance to any financial provider company or employer. Otherwise, that representative may be under pressure, if not required, to sell preselected products without regard to what is truly in the client's best interest.

- **Licensed in both insurance and securities** without limitation. If your financial representative is licensed in only one area, that person may be biased toward the industry they can sell for and against the one they cannot.

- **Has a non-exclusive cooperative relationship** with other professionals (e.g., attorney, CPA, etc.) and is willing to meet with those professionals with the client, not simply make a "blind referral."

How Advisors Are Compensated:

Insurance licensed professionals (called Agents) are compensated by commission. In most cases, that commission payment comes directly from the issuing company and does not come from the client's money. In other words, the agent is paid from the same pool of money that pays all the employees at the insurance company.

Investment licensed professionals (called Registered Representatives or registered Investment Advisors depending on license type) are paid from whatever investment fees are imposed, whether loads (e.g., Mutual Funds), transaction-based fees or asset management fees. In some cases, these costs may be negotiable and in others not. Discuss details with your investment rep or advisor.

Fee-for-service (from Registered Investment Advisors only). As with other highly skilled, licensed professionals (Accountants, Attorneys, etc.) clients pay for professional advice without regard to products that are purchased. The value of a fee-for-service arrangement is that the advisor has no artificial bias or motivation to recommend one product over another. The disadvantage is that a customer must pay for the advice and then pay for the product anyway.

Regardless of the type of advisor you select, you want to think about that person as heading a team of professionals rather than one of many separate professionals operating without communication or consideration to the others. You may think "*I don't have a big enough estate to warrant all that.*"

Unfortunately, that thinking may be backwards. Don't believe me? Ask yourself the following question: "*Who would be harmed more by losing $100,000: you or a billionaire?*"

So who needs financial planning with their IRAs? The answer is anyone who wants to maximize benefits to them and not the IRS.

ABOUT THE AUTHOR

MICHAEL TOVE holds a Ph.D. in behavioral biology who in 1996, made a career shift into insurance and financial services. In that capacity, he is both insurance and securities licensed, a Certified Estate Planner, a Registered Financial Consultant, and a Registered Investment Advisor with CoreCap Investment Advisors, Inc. In 1998, he founded AIN Services as a fully independent financial planning firm located near Raleigh, North Carolina. AIN Services and CoreCap are separate and unaffiliated businesses. He is a member of the National Institute of Certified Estate Planners, the International Association of Registered Financial Consultants and the Independent Excellence Group, a by invitation-only financial think-tank organization. He is a regular contributing author in the professional and popular financial literature and past co-host of the TV show *Money Secrets with Bill and Mike*. He has previously authored two books on financial matters: *What You Don't Know About Retirement Income Can Hurt You* (2015) for which he wrote two chapters and *Money Secrets with Bill and Mike* (2017) by Michael Tove and Bill Alexander. You can contact Dr. Tove by visiting his website www.AIN-Services.com.

www.ingramcontent.com/pod-product-compliance
Lightning Source LLC
Chambersburg PA
CBHW060614210326
41520CB00010B/1328